Call #
DA960.I59 1999

LCCN
2004484781

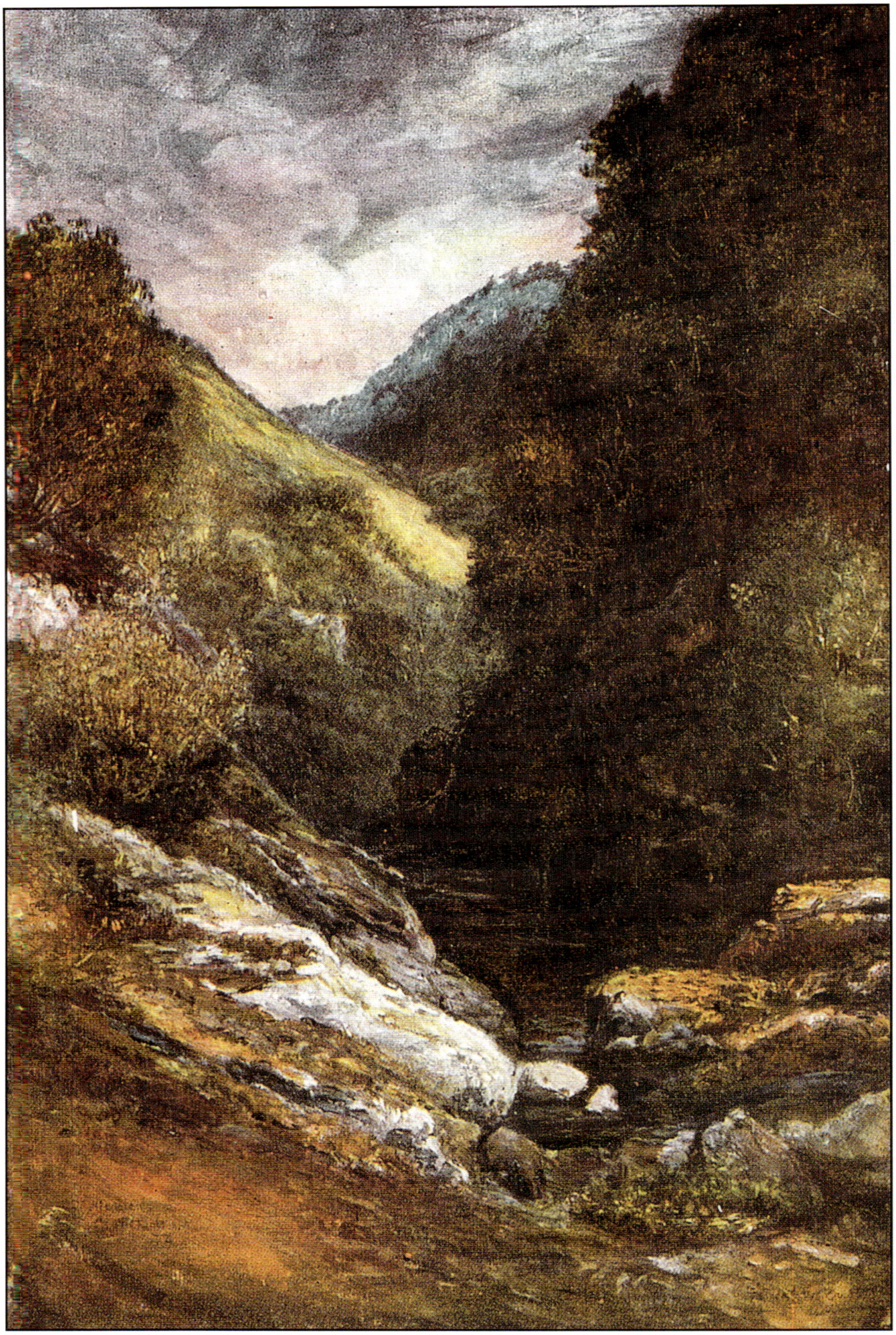

The Way Things Were

IRELAND

The Emerald Isle

Edited by Andrew Pagett

Illustrated by Francis S. Walker

BROCKHAMPTON PRESS

Ireland - The Emerald Isle

First published by Brockhampton Press Ltd
20 Bloomsbury Street
London WC1B 3QA

© Brockhampton Press Ltd, 1999

ISBN 1 86019 934 8

All rights reserved. No part of this publication
may be reproduced, stored in a retrieval
system, or transmitted in any form
or by any means, electronic, mechanical,
photocopying, recording or
otherwise, without the
prior permission of
the copyright owners.

Conceived and designed by Savitri Books Ltd

Printed and bound by
APP Printing, Singapore

CONTENTS

Introduction..8

A Land of Contradictions..10

Donegal..22

Across Lough Foyle..34

Within the Pale..44

Connaught..58

South from Dublin..70

South-East and South-West..80

The Islands..112

Saints and Sinners..120

Frontispiece picture:

THE DEVIL'S GLEN, WICKLOW

A rocky gorge about 300 feet deep and thickly wooded, through which flows
the Vartry river. This sketch was taken at the head of the Glen
over the waterfall.

INTRODUCTION

Francis S. Walker was born in County Meath in 1848. At the age of twenty he moved to London to study art and he lived mostly in London for the rest of his life. Like many of his contemporary artists he first earned his living as an illustrator before exhibiting his work at the Royal Academy and later concentrating on mezzotinting and etching his own paintings.

As the illustrations in this book show, he never lost his love of his native land. It shines out of his studies of landscape, buildings and, above all, people. Walker's portrait of Ireland depicts a romantic, untroubled land – a picture that is strangely at variance with the facts of Irish history. The country has seen a succession of invaders – Danes, Normans and wave upon wave of English and Scots. But even when these were successful in military and economic terms, they never succeeded in suppressing the indomitable Irish spirit.

The text is drawn largely from the writings of Frank Mathew, barrister and novelist, a native of Tipperary, who explained this paradox in a very straightforward way: the invaders, for the most part, simply 'became Irish'. Mathew was writing in the early years of the twentieth century, when Ireland was officially one nation, governed from Westminster, and he chose not to dwell on the struggle for Home Rule that dominated Irish politics at that time. Instead he provides a vivid, poetic and entertaining picture of Ireland and the Irish people as they battled not only against political and religious oppression, but against each other for the fun of it and against the elements and the landscape that shaped their lives.

St Kevin's Church, Glendalough, County Wicklow

Sir Walter Scott described it as 'the inestimably singular scene of Irish antiquity'. The church, which goes back to the sixth century, is a fine example of a double-vaulted oratory, resembling that of Kells.

A LAND OF CONTRADICTIONS

There have been many names for Ireland. The fishermen of Connemara talk of an island just off their western coast, not to be found by any voyage. It is a country both near and remote; they call it 'the Other Country'. This is a term that could equally well be employed for Ireland itself. One early writer believed that Ireland was 'separated from the rest of the known world, and in some sort to be distinguished as another world'; other names from the past include 'the Oldest Place' and 'the Country at the End of the Earth'.

In ancient times the belief in this 'Other Country', 'the Island of the Blessed', brought comfort to the living, because they felt that their dead were happy and near; they in their turn hoped that they would find eternal happiness within sight of their earthly homes. A more recent view suggests that the sorrows of this life continued on the island, and brought the dead back to attend to former concerns. One solitary old man who had cared for nothing but his sheep was frequently seen, a year after his death, guiding his flock over the mountain, because the drunken youngster who had replaced him fell asleep and left the sheep to wander; in another variation on the theme the spirit of a young mother was said to return to soothe her crying child in the night, taking it up in her cold arms and, once it was peacefully asleep, returning quietly whence she had come.

This sort of contradiction is typical of Ireland. It is a land of paradoxes. Frequently known as the Island of Saints, it has produced its share of sinners.

Salmon-fishing in Connemara

Its people have always been rightly renowned for courage, yet that quality has procured them little success. Its spell has conquered its innumerable conquerors – yet how can that appeal be called Irishness, when so many stocks blend to make up the Irish? The country has been haunted by trouble, yet there are those (perhaps especially in England) who would say it had given not inconsiderable trouble in return.

There are contradictions, too, in Irish Christianity. In happy co-existence with the fervent belief in saints is the deeply ingrained faith in the Irish Fairyland, Tyranoge. As Frank Mathew wrote in 1904:

> Other races have known fairies and elves, but none with the same intimate and enduring affection. While others have forgotten these beliefs, the Irish have retained them more eagerly than you might imagine if you were to judge by the little you hear on the subject. Fear of ridicule may stop a grown man speaking of the Fairies, but the restraint is also imposed by his respect for their feelings – it is well known that they do not like to be mentioned, so anyone who speaks of them must be careful to call them the Little Good People. The Fairies are Irish, and therefore embody the contradictions of the Irish character: they are pleasure-loving and quarrelsome, kindly, dangerous and peculiarly sensitive. Dwelling in a bright land of peace under the hills, the Fairies are immortal and untroubled and innocent.

The certainty that so pleasant a land and so carefree a life were so near brought rest and consolation to many whose lot was different. It was not everyone who could behold the Little Good People, but many were cheered by glimpses of them, and saw them playing football with dead leaves, or dancing on the green hill-tops by the light of the moon.

The monks, on the other hand, were seen everywhere and by everyone. The ruins of monasteries could be found in the dark heart of the mountains and

Castle Caldwell on the Borders of Lough Erne

in the pleasant rolling hills. This is perhaps a token of the phases through which Christianity passed here. When it was first preached, it won the hearts of the Celts because it taught self-denial and was founded on sorrow. Old poems contrast the joyous life of the Fenians, the legendary people said to have inhabited Ireland in prehistoric times, with the austerity introduced by St Patrick. But by the time Christianity had come to be part of the Irish nature, it was no longer associated with penitence; it was a fountain of perpetual gladness.

Ireland is also the Island of Ruins. To look at it, underpopulated and impoverished, you might think that its condition was the work of a conqueror who left devastation in his wake and called it Peace, and this theory would seem to be supported by the number of ruins, for in every part there are the wrecks of old castles, churches, abbeys and the desolate homes of the poor; but this is a deceptive appearance: those who enquire into the history of these remnants learn that many of them were made by the Irish, and that others were merely left to decay.

Irish landscapes are often made to look all the more unfortunate by the bare walls of roofless cabins among the hedges or alone on the hills; each speaks of hearths grown cold and families vanished. Many were once tenanted by people who afterwards emigrated – and not always of their own volition, as we shall see. But the full truth is that these cabins survived as wrecks as a

Opposite:

Blarney Castle

'The lovely groves and grounds,' Francis Walker wrote, 'had more interest for me
than the structure itself. However, I thought I must kiss the Blarney stone,
and proceeded to the top of the castle, about eighty feet high; I found
the stone was about four or five feet down from the top, and that it
would be necessary to stoop over, head down, and hold on by the legs.
Seeing me hesitate, a man asked me: "Are you afraid?" "I am."

"Well, no man that's afeard ought to go a-kissing. All kissing should be done sudden; when you hesitate it's serious. Make way for that young lady, she's not afraid." The feat accomplished, he cried out, "A cheer for the young English lady." "No," she replied, "Amurrican!"

result of Irish ways. The Irish peasant preferred to build a shed for himself rather than use one in which some other family had suffered, for he did not wish to be haunted by its former inhabitants or its ancient ill luck. Because the cabins were rudimentary they were cheap to construct, and there was no need to pull down the old ones, since the fields were abundantly provided with stones to serve as building materials. Also, it was unlucky to take stones from the dead. This belief guarded the ivied hulks of castles, too, while those of ecclesiastical buildings were further protected by veneration.

In addition, the peasant saw that if the walls of a former cottage were kept standing, they would prove useful as shelters for cattle, or for men caught in storms. For all these reasons he left them alone, not feeling that they were unsightly or out of place. Nor were they, for the weather of Ireland soon tinted them, and they quickly seemed only too natural; they endowed that silent country with much of its mournful attraction.

Ireland has also often been called the Green Isle or the Emerald Isle. The latter name was first used by Dr Drennan in his poem *Erin*:

> Nor one feeling of vengeance presume to defile
> The cause or the men of the Emerald Isle.

But this appellation, although it has become very popular, is not entirely accurate, as Mathew explained:

> If you have not visited Ireland, the odds are that you think its landscape wholly addicted to the wearing of the Green. Why else would it be called the Green Isle? Yet few of the pictures in this book show green as the prominent colour – many of them capture varying shades of brown. Most of Ireland has the colouring of a wood in the autumn. In the wide places of bogs and in the Highlands, it is mostly brown, although the shades change as the

GLENDALOUGH

An additional attraction is lent to the sombre beauty of the Upper Lake, Glandalough, by the legend attached to St Kevin's bed, a cavity halfway up the side of the cliff, and difficult of access. Those who achieve this feat are told that if they wish for anything while there, it will be granted within the year.

sky changes above them, and seem at times to be purple or red or black: the smaller hills are grey, and so are the moors. There *is* green here, but it is hidden; lurking behind the more obvious hues as it does in the wood just before the leaves fall. One is always aware of green, though sometimes without seeing it. It is as if it were implied. The grey of the hills may remind you of a mist over leaves. Though there are some valleys in which the verdure resembles moss, it is more often wan and elusive. England, which has so many more woods and meadows, has in truth a far greater right to be called the Green Isle.

Ireland was once the Island of Woods, but it is bare now. Its greenness is ghostly, as if it were haunted by the spirits of the branches that covered it once. Throughout Ireland – and throughout the pictures in this book – you will see delicate light, making the colours subdued and remote, with a purity that elsewhere belongs only to the very early morning. In this, as in other things, Ireland is a country apart.

The scantest understanding of Irish history will make the reader aware of the almost constant conflict that has taken place in Ireland over the centuries. The early mythology is full of clans and heroes and bloody battles, of clubs that can slay nine men at a stroke and special brews that made the drinker

Opposite

The Round Tower on Devenish Island

Situated on Lough Erne, about two miles from Enniskillen, this is said to be one of the finest towers in Ireland. Near it are the remains of two churches, around which are burial grounds. At the time Francis Walker painted this scene, these cemeteries were still in use and the funerals held there were said to be impressive, with the body being brought to the island by a procession of boats from the Port of Lamentation, in Portora, Enniskillen.

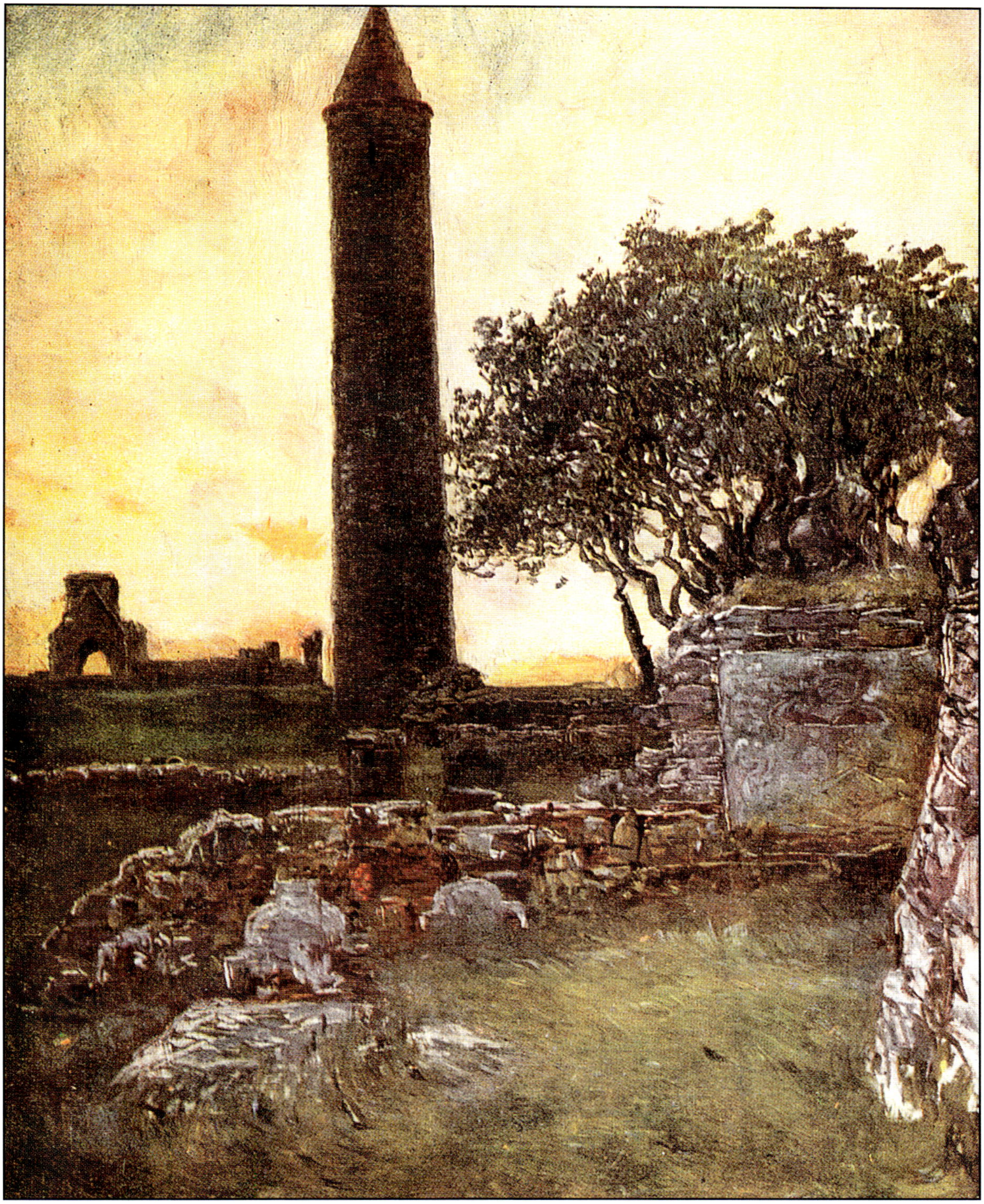

invincible in war. The people living in Ireland in Roman times, the Celts or Gaels, were, according to the historian Tacitus, much superior to the Britons in culture and character, yet they were divided into miniature nations perpetually at war. Introduced to Christianity by St Patrick in the fifth century, they took to it willingly, sending out missionaries to the still barbarous British mainland and converting their pagan Mother Goddess Brigid into a saint. Over the next few hundred years their sea-going trade was controlled by the Danes, who in the course of time conquered parts of Ireland and founded new cities and kingdoms – the names Waterford and Wexford, among many others, still attest their Danish ancestry.

The next invaders were Norman knights, who found the country divided as England had not been for many centuries and carved out little realms for themselves. Then the English left Ireland pretty much alone until Tudor times, when the Protestant Queen Elizabeth attempted a conquest whose resistance was aided by the Pope and Catholic Spain – turning the conflict into a religious war. The large-scale English and Scottish settlement of Ireland began at this time, with resistance firmly suppressed, most notoriously by Oliver Cromwell in 1649–50. After this, much Irish land was confiscated and given to the settlers, paving the way for centuries of political and economic ascendancy of the Protestant minority. Forty years after Cromwell, William III of England (the former Prince William of Orange) defeated the supporters of the deposed Catholic King James II at the Battle of the Boyne, and introduced the first anti-Catholic laws.

This book is a work neither of history nor of politics, though it is impossible to avoid either when painting a lifelike portrait of Ireland. It is not the writer's intention to discuss more recent events and conflicts. Rather it is his aim to convey something of the spell of Ireland which, despite everything, subdued so many of its conquerors and made even them choose to consider themselves Irish. If Ireland is frequently misunderstood, it is perhaps because of these Irish peculiarities. Ireland is, above all, a land of contradictions.

INNISFALLEN

Sweet Innisfallen, long shall dwell
    In memory's dream that sunny smile
Which over thee on that evening fell
    When first I saw thy fairy isle.
              (*Thomas Moore*)

DONEGAL

The name of this remote nook amid the mountains of the north means Fort of the Strangers. In fact Donegal has always been the fort of the Irish, those perpetual strangers; the one area in which there has been no challenge to their right to occupy and rule. Cut off from the rest of the country by barren, mountainous country, it was not a place that attracted covetous conquerors. It was included, of course, in the Partition of Ireland, when Oliver Cromwell tried to herd the Irish people into Connaught while distributing the rest of the country among his own followers (of which unhappy event we shall hear more later in this book). Donegal was one of the many areas he bestowed on those who had served under him, but they were not pleased with it: its rough terrain was no good for would-be farmers, and it cut them off too mercilessly from friends and family.

Nor, apparently, were they favourably impressed with the people they found there. This is understandable – the men of Donegal were not unexpectedly hostile because their land had been taken from them and bestowed on these intruders and, once winter made the dark valleys that separated them from the outside world impassable, it must have felt all the more unwelcoming to the newcomers. So the few veterans who bothered to travel to this distant land went back to their comrades with unenthusiastic reports, and in the Fort of the Strangers Cromwell's schemes largely failed. The shares he had assigned were sold cheaply, and although the original inhabitants were forced to acknowledge new landlords, they continued to a large extent undisturbed. Unlike the rest of the Irish, therefore, their blood remained pure, and their character deserves particular study as being the most representative of the Irish as they were before the English infiltration.

HARVEST-TIME IN DONEGAL

'The road from Doochary Bridge to Fintown crosses a very wild district,
where life seems barely possible,' Francis Walker wrote in 1904,
'yet I saw a piece of land created by being dug out of a bog, surrounded
on all sides by high rocks; it was built up out of the water and levelled
on the top, and a crop of corn was subsequently sown and reaped upon it.
To my mind, a remarkable example of the industry
and thrift of the people'.

Although unadulterated by 'foreign' stock, the Donegal character has perhaps been modified by enforced peace. In the old days this land was called Tir-Connell (Donegal was only the name of a little fort set under mountains at the head of a long sheltered bay) and in this wild refuge the warlike O'Donnells held sway. But all the clans of the region were great fighters – the annals of other distant counties record their devastating raids. Once those pursuits, naturally congenial to the native of Donegal, were barred, his character must gradually have become subdued. The silence of their desolate homeland must have seemed strange to men accustomed to the wailing whoops of war cries and the piercing note of the pipes.

Yet while making allowances for the passing of many peaceful centuries, it seems reasonable to infer that these Highlanders still greatly resemble the fierce, kilted warriors who paid homage to the legendary leader known as the Dark Daughter and her fearsome son, Red Hugh. The ruins of Kilbarron Castle, between Donegal and Ballyshannon, still speak of its former masters, the O'Clerys, whose exploits feature in ancient annals; in the same area are to be found the ruins of many abbeys and colleges. For much as these warlike clans honoured valour, they honoured piety yet more.

A map dating from the time of Queen Elizabeth gave the invaders a bloody idea of the men they were to meet. It indicates the territory of each clan by displaying the arms of its chief. Most notably, Owen Oge of the Battle-axe is depicted in the full regalia of a savage leader. This is perhaps not surprising, as Her Majesty's Deputies (the English Ministers sent to rule Ireland) were concerned only with the question of whether or not Owen was likely to wield his battle-axe; they knew little and cared less about the men he commanded. But these grim chiefs, all-powerful in their day, are now commemorated only by name; it is not they who are revered by the people of Donegal.

For instance, there is in the high cliffs by Horn Head a cave through which the sea plunges in storms with a noise like the report of a cannon; it is called MacSwiney's Gun. It is easy to speculate on the reputation of the now forgotten

WASHING DAY IN THE WEST OF IRELAND

Francis Walker's picture shows a peasant woman washing clothes by the side of a running stream, with water put to boil on a turf fire.

MacSwiney, but the average native of Donegal will know little about him than that. But ask such a man about the great Donegal saint, Columba, and you will find that he has the details of his life at his fingertips, although Columba's bones had crumbled into dust a thousand years before the birth of MacSwiney.

Columba was born by Lough Gartan in the year 521. He became a monk and built his first monastery at Daire Calgach, the Oak Grove of Calgach, a place afterwards called in his honour Daire Columbkille, and later, having passed under another influence, Londonderry. Columba's religious zeal might have been enough to keep his memory alive, but the persistence of his fame is due to his warlike exploits. Learning that a neighbouring king possessed an illuminated copy of the Gospels, he asked for a copy, but was refused. When he obtained one by stealth it was claimed by the original owner and Columba's refusal led to bloody war. Neither side being victorious in battle, the issue was submitted to Cormac, King of Meath, who banished Columba from Ireland until such time as he had saved as many souls as had been killed in the war.

Arriving thereafter on the Scottish island of Iona, Columba founded still another monastery, whence he embarked on the task of converting the Picts to Christianity. He was a lover of peace, but always ready to fight if occasion was given. He was a just man who hated and would not tolerate injustice. A poet, a scholar, a builder, a complex mix of hot-bloodedness and tranquillity, completely indefatigable, a skilled seaman and great traveller who passionately loved his home and – these combinations and contradictions make him a true son of Donegal, and today's sons of Donegal recognise this, continuing to love and honour his memory when those who led more exemplary lives are forgotten.

Opposite:

St Columbkille's Cross, Kells

This ancient cross is one of several to be found in the town. Walker remarked on the interesting carvings which adorned its surface.

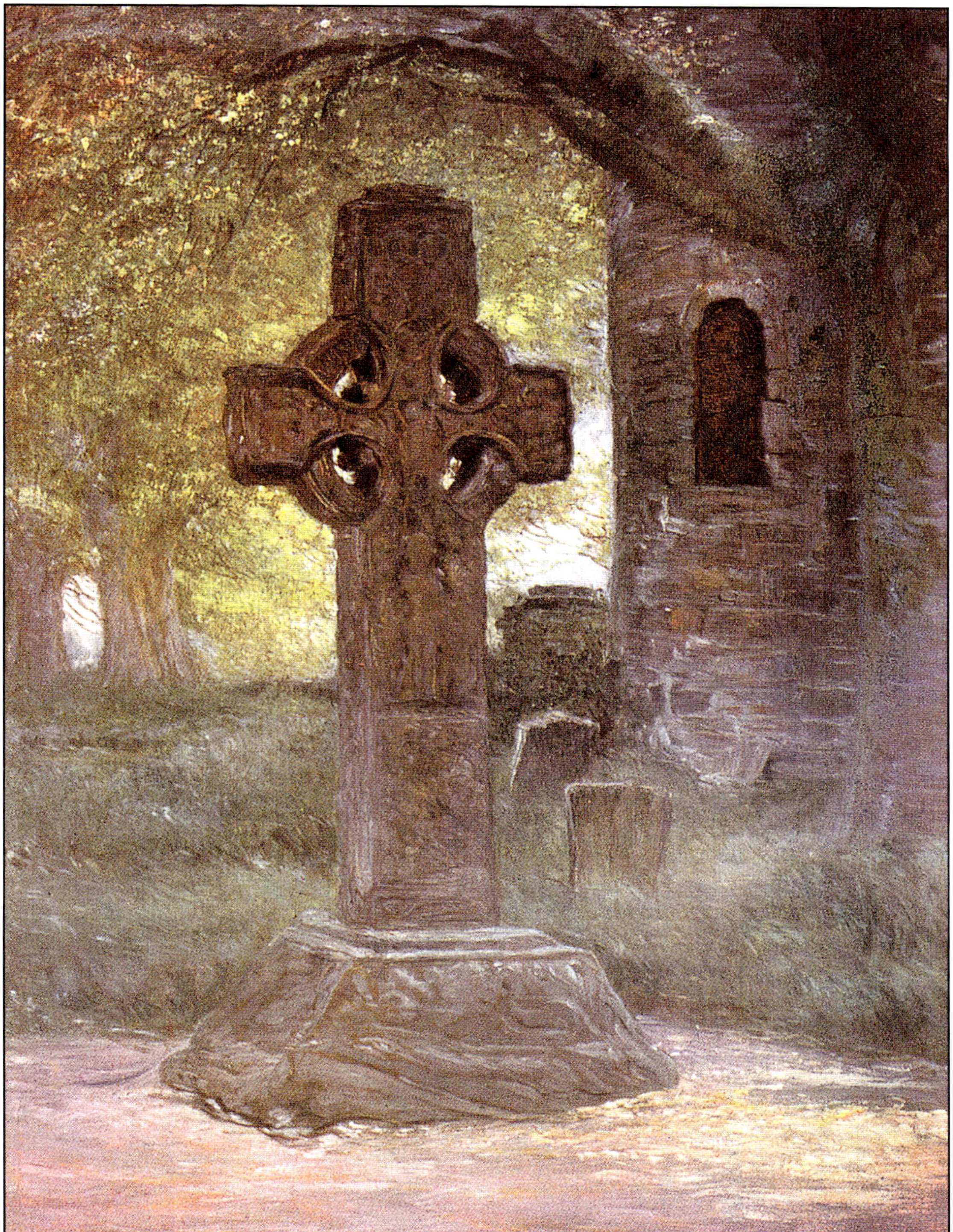

On a hill over Lough Gartan there is a long slab of rock called Ethne's Bed on which Columba's mother is said to have lain while he was born; and it is believed that those who sleep on it will be protected against homesickness for ever. Many of the teeming thousands who left Donegal to try for better times in America are said to have spent a night here under the stars. The story goes that Columba, sick with longing for his wild home in even wilder Iona, prayed that future generations of his fellow countrymen be immune from the grief he was suffering; and the persistence of the belief shows how that love of home is understood and carried on by his people.

Intimately associated though Columba is with Gartan, the place that bears his name is some distance away, above Malinmore Head, where the heavy waves roll in from the west. It is from here that he is said to have set sail for Iona after the judgement of Cormac went against him. Glen Columbkille is a strangely calm place, though the call of the sea echoes through it. Often prayers and hymns echo through it, too, for it is a favourite haunt of pilgrims. But the place was hallowed before Columba was born. Dark little hovels, of a date earlier than his, are scattered over it. Stone circles are found all over the area, and it seems certain that here, as elsewhere, Columba sanctified a site that had once been holy to the Druids. The glen itself feels as if it had been sacred since time immemorial: it is like a vast church whose roof is the sky. From within its depth the sound of the sea and the voices of the pilgrims are muted and serve only to remind you that silence is absolute here.

Glen Columbkille is the heart of Donegal. If you wish to know the hearts of the people, you can best understand them in this solitude. The neighbouring cliffs are sheer walls. Glen Head stands erect, 800 feet high, dwarfed by the precipitous flank of Slieve League over Carrick. From the brink of Slieve League the waves flash 1800 feet below. The granite walls by the seas are grimly defensive. Yet many smooth strands are beneath them, and they shelter many calm inlets, such as Lough Swilly, the Lake of Shadows. Although the name comes from the physical shadows, it is justified also by the memories of the chiefs of Tir-Connell. Many were the battles they fought beside it. Red

HORN HEAD, DONEGAL

The Head gets its name from the horn-like rocks which rise more than 600 feet from the sea.

Hugh, that firebrand of the mountains, was captured on it in his boyhood, and it was made famous by the Flight of the Earls. Down to the shore, on a dark September morning in 1607, came the great Earl of Tyrone and his comrade the Earl of Tyr-Connell, when, having abandoned hope of resisting the latest wave of invaders, they forsook Ireland for ever. Their long struggle over, there remained only a brief period of exile in defeat before they were laid to rest where the Church of San Pietro in Montorio looks over Rome. From the quiet waters of Lough Swilly they passed away and became shadows.

But the din of those battles and the passionate laments of that morning did not break the peace of this haven. They were momentary; this is eternal. In all these indomitable Highlands you feel that there is peace at the core. Those savage ramparts protect the level sands, the shadowy bays and the peaceful hollows; the sternest and the wildest of all guard Glen Columbkille.

Frank Mathew had this to say about the Highlanders of Donegal:

> They are a hardy race and a taciturn one, moulded by solitude and a sea-faring life. Because they live among rocks, they have to brave the North Atlantic in the quest for food, or cross rough seas to cut the harvests of strangers. They do this willingly enough, for they have been strengthened by the invigorating air; here you will find none of the terror with which the fishermen of Connemara regard the ocean, nor will you observe their despairing melancholy. If the people of Donegal have a melancholy look, you feel that their sadness is a pleasure to them, and a wholesome one. They have the brave pride of independence.
>
> In no land will you see a more dignified hospitality. Even the poorest man is proud of his home, and with good reason, for, however lowly it may be, it represents infinite toil. You will find crops growing in unnatural places, on the sandy edges of cliffs and up in the mountains between clusters of rocks, and you will learn

SLIEVE LEAGUE – THE MOUNTAIN OF THE FLAG STONES

From Bunglass Point the view of the southern face of Slieve League, which rises
abruptly from the sea to the height of 1889 feet, if once see,
can never be forgotten. The cliffs here are said to be the highest in Europe,
and, in the opinion of the late Lord Leighton, who painted them
as background to many of his classic compositions,
the most impressive.

that some of these high fields have been made by the simple process of carrying the soil from beneath. You will see young girls digging potatoes, or tugging the fishing nets, or carrying heavy baskets on their backs up the long mountain paths; and the rough cabins sing with the murmur of looms. Here the old ways of extracting dyes from the heather are followed, and so are the old methods of weaving that are not to be rivalled by any machine.

Faced with evidence of such industry, one might expect comparative wealth; but that is not to be found. This is one of the poorest peoples on the face of the earth, and one of the happiest. Hard though their life is, it is lit by an inner content. Though their home is so stern, they can imagine no worse calamity than to be exiled from it. Life is full of labour for them, but the peace of Glen Columbkille abides in their hearts.

There is in these Highlands a singular freshness. It is as if the air had been kept from any taint by the barrier that holds them secluded. It is no wonder that its people are choked by the thick air of other lands and long to return, even though they have slept on Ethne's Bed under the stars. Neither can they find anywhere else a country more beautiful, for, wild though it is, it has a magical colouring, and if that is subdued it lends the more charm to the vivid face of the sea. You will never forget Horn Head if you see it on a bright, windy morning, when the many colours scurry across it and beneath it the sea flashes with blue and green and silver, and the long yellow sands of Tramore glitter like gold.

Opposite:

A Home in Donegal

In many of the peasants' home in the north of Ireland the weaving of cloth and carpets was carried out by the men. The women did the spinning and dyeing, so that the whole family shared in the work, which was often very beautiful, both in colouring and quality.

ACROSS LOUGH FOYLE

Nature kept Tir-Connell away from hostile Tir-Owen by interposing placid Lough Foyle. At the time when the era of the clans was drawing to a close, the O'Donnells were lords on one side of that long, sheltered bay, and the O'Neills on the other. There were minor chiefs, too, who held sway over their own peoples: Inishowen, the dark country between Lough Foyle and Lough Swilly, was ruled by the O'Dochertys and the opposite hills by the O'Connells; but the two greater houses overshadowed these lesser fiefdoms and acknowledged no rivals except those dangerous Scots, the MacDonnells of Antrim. Centuries later, Lough Foyle continued its role of keeping hostile forces apart – this time the Celtic and Catholic part of the north from the Protestant 'colonised' one.

Even the country is different once you have crossed Lough Foyle and left Donegal behind. It is a castellated coast. Tory Island was named Torach, the Island of Towers, because of its high broken cliffs, and this coast could earn the same name. Instead of the solid granite fortifications of Donegal, there are shattered black buttresses and towers of basalt. If you glimpse the coast from the sea, you are more likely to think that these are strongholds in ruins than to recognise them for the natural defences that they are. Indeed, it is said that the galleons of the Spanish Armada made that mistake and bombarded the cliffs.

Old legends assert that the cliffs owe their shape to the workings of the Devil, who fashioned them with intent to deceive; others suggest that the rocky turrets and battlements were crafted by giants, who were once populous in

A CORACLE, TORY ISLAND

The coracle or curragh varied in shape on various parts of the coast. At Galway it resembled a section of a walnut shell, but in Donegal a high prow was required to resist the great waves of this wild coast. Coracles were very light, without a keel and built on a frame with wicker sides, which was covered with skin or tarred canvas.

these parts. One of them, known as Balor of the Mighty Blows, is said to have inhabited Tory Island and was doubly redoubtable because he had an eye in the back of his head. Then there was the chivalrous one who took the trouble to build the Giant's Causeway, arranging its unnatural tiers so that another giant, who lived in Scotland, could come over and fight him without inconvenience.

Interwoven with these towers are others built by mortal men, the stark ruins of castles perched high among the natural turrets, as if they had been meant to be out of harm's way, but nonetheless shattered long ago and abandoned to the fury of the storms. These ruins are inseparable from the cliffs that dominate them. Even the proudest of them all, Dunluce Castle, looming out of the mist from its high separated rock, might easily be mistaken for part of the ruined sea-wall behind it. Perhaps it is true that only a giant could have placed it there.

Inland the country is also quite unlike that of Donegal. Here you are no longer in mountains; as you go eastwards you see the hills dwindle and the land become fertile. Once you reach the part that faces Scotland, this gentleness extends down to the sea. The savage and fantastical defences of the west never penetrated here, leaving the coast comparatively low and unguarded. This more vulnerable coastline continued along most of the east coast of Ireland, so that the land that lay closest to Scotland and England was the most approachable part of the country and thus the most readily colonised. The mountains, of course, were left to the Celts: even in Protestant Antrim there has always been a Celtic and Catholic fringe along the cliffs on the north.

The level parts of Antrim and Down were always attractive to foreigners. The Danes found their way there; so did the Normans and the Highland Scots who, though a kindred race, were nonetheless regarded as aliens. Whether or not the steps of the Giant's Causeway ever extended to the opposite Highlands, there was always traffic across the water that separated

TRAMORE STRAND

This desolate outcrop is close to Tory Island, which can be seen on the horizon,
nine miles off. Francis Walker recalled that at some point the inhabitants
had been unable to pay rent, so a gunboat was sent to remove them
to the workhouse on the mainland. It was wrecked on the rocks,
and further attempts at removing the inhabitants were abandonned.
The rent was allegedly still unpaid when Walker
recorded this scene.

them. Then the Scottish MacDonnells of the Isles took possession of a territory in Antrim, and afterwards of Rathlin Island, that pile of black and white basalt off its northern coast, and other barren and inhospitable tracts. Randal MacDonnell, first Lord of Antrim, was permitted to keep this land when 40,000 more desirable acres were sold to London companies following the Flight of the Earls.

It was in that year – 1607 – that the history of the Protestant North of Ireland began. The O'Neills had been Lords of Tir-Owen, the country between Lough Erne and the mouth of the Lagan River, from time immemorial. Like the O'Donnells, they had been at their greatest as the period of their dominance was drawing near its close. Shane the Proud, the first Earl of Tyrone, had put himself forward as a candidate for the Crown of All Ireland, and might have secured it if his countrymen had sided with him. The second and greater Earl of Tyrone had joined forces with his rival, Red Hugh of the O'Donnells, and had shaken the grip of England again; but after his many wars he had knelt in homage to a dead woman. The news of Queen Elizabeth's death had been kept from him lest at the last moment he refused to yield. But the Earl of Tyrone had fallen, and doomed himself to that miserable exile in Rome. The Catholic and rebellious O'Neills ruled Tir-Owen no more. Before long, the city at the mouth of the Lagan River was Ireland's most flourishing monument to Protestant loyalism. That city is today called Belfast.

Beal-na-Farsad, the Mouth of the Ford, was merely a name until a castle was built there by De Courcy, one of the first Norman adventurers. The first castle soon burned down, but was restored and in 1612 granted to Lord Chichester, who became first Baron of Belfast. He built a small town and imported many staunch Presbyterians from the lowlands of Scotland. These men made Belfast. It has long attracted strangers who, like so many others who settled in Ireland, soon become Irish and paradoxically achieved a deep love of their adopted country, while retaining their dislike of its older inhabitants.

MOUNT ERRIGAL

The shape of this mountain probably indicates a volcanic origin.
It is the highest point in Donnegal.

If Lough Foyle had managed to separate Catholic from Protestant entirely, the Protestant North might soon have become peaceful. But a few Catholics refused to be ousted and Catholic outposts such as Derry-Columbkille remained – comparatively secure from invading forces because they were on the west side of Lough Foyle. The Scottish and English colonisation of these counties after 1612 led to long years of war. In the course of time some of the colonists founded a secret society called the Peep o' Day Boys, so named because they formed the habit of calling upon their Catholic neighbours at dawn and giving them the option of departing 'to Hell or to Connaught' – that distant county to which Cromwell was soon to exile all the Irish. In retaliation the Catholic peasants formed themselves into a similarly belligerent organisation known as the Defenders.

Through all this Belfast – a hive of industrial activity – prospered. There are those who maintain that these northern counties succeeded commercially because their people were of Protestant and Scottish ancestry. But Mathew maintained that this was false.

> Their industry and vigour are due to the different air of the North, and that is why you find it equally in wild Donegal; it is just that the remoteness and lack of organisation in Donegal provide lesser rewards for one's efforts. Determined, hard-working people are as much in evidence among Irish Catholics in Antrim or Down as they are in the Protestant enclaves. Some of the chief manufacturers are of Irish descent, and the best qualities of the North have been seen in such Catholics as Lord Russell of Killowen, the prominent lawyer and Liberal MP who ended his career as Lord Chief Justice.

That said, the advantages that accrued from the settlers' being Scottish and Protestant cannot be dismissed. The Scots settled quickly and happily into their new home for the simple reason that it was not dissimilar to their old one. Nor was it at any great distance from it; from Irish shores the Scots

Killowen

could see the land of their birth. Because they were Protestants, they were united against their Catholic neighbours, for they landed in Ireland at a time when the two religions were everywhere openly hostile to each other. But the Protestants were more fortunate than the Catholics of Ireland, in that their history began only in 1612; they had no long years of bitter subjection to recall, no imagined past bliss to lament. Unity and a common belief in danger endowed them with strength, and in all their dealings they exhibited the ready and masterful spirit of soldiers. The colonised North prospered at least in part because it was the Fort of the Strangers.

Opposite:

A Fair

In this picture, Francis Walker recorded the Irish custom of slapping the open hand of the other party to a deal in token of agreement.

If both parties proved to be unusually obstinate, a friendly neighbour would sometimes intervene and place their hands together, offering advice on how to break the deadlock.

WITHIN THE PALE

South of County Down begins the part of Ireland longest held by England and once called the English Pale. When in the twelfth century King Henry II saw the success of the first of his Norman knights who had chosen to venture to Ireland, he thought it was time to assert his claim to a part of the spoils, but did not wish to attempt the conquest of the country himself. Instead he gave his subjects leave to subdue the wilder parts at their own risk and expense. At the same time declaring himself overlord, he took possession of Dublin and of a long narrow tract of the country round it. This, he reasoned, would be the royal foothold from which at some future time he or a later King of England could conquer the rest of Ireland, after private adventurers had broken its strength. He gave orders, it is said, that a moat should be dug along the inner side of his new territory, and that this boundary should be studded with castles.

Opposite:

A Holy Well

Tubernalty is situated at the head of Lough Gill and from it flows a stream of clear water. Walker's picture shows a small altar decked with vases of flowers and candles. He observed that many pilgrims came to the well and drank the water. Some took off their shoes and headgear, walked around the well three times, then lit the candles, while saying a few prayers.

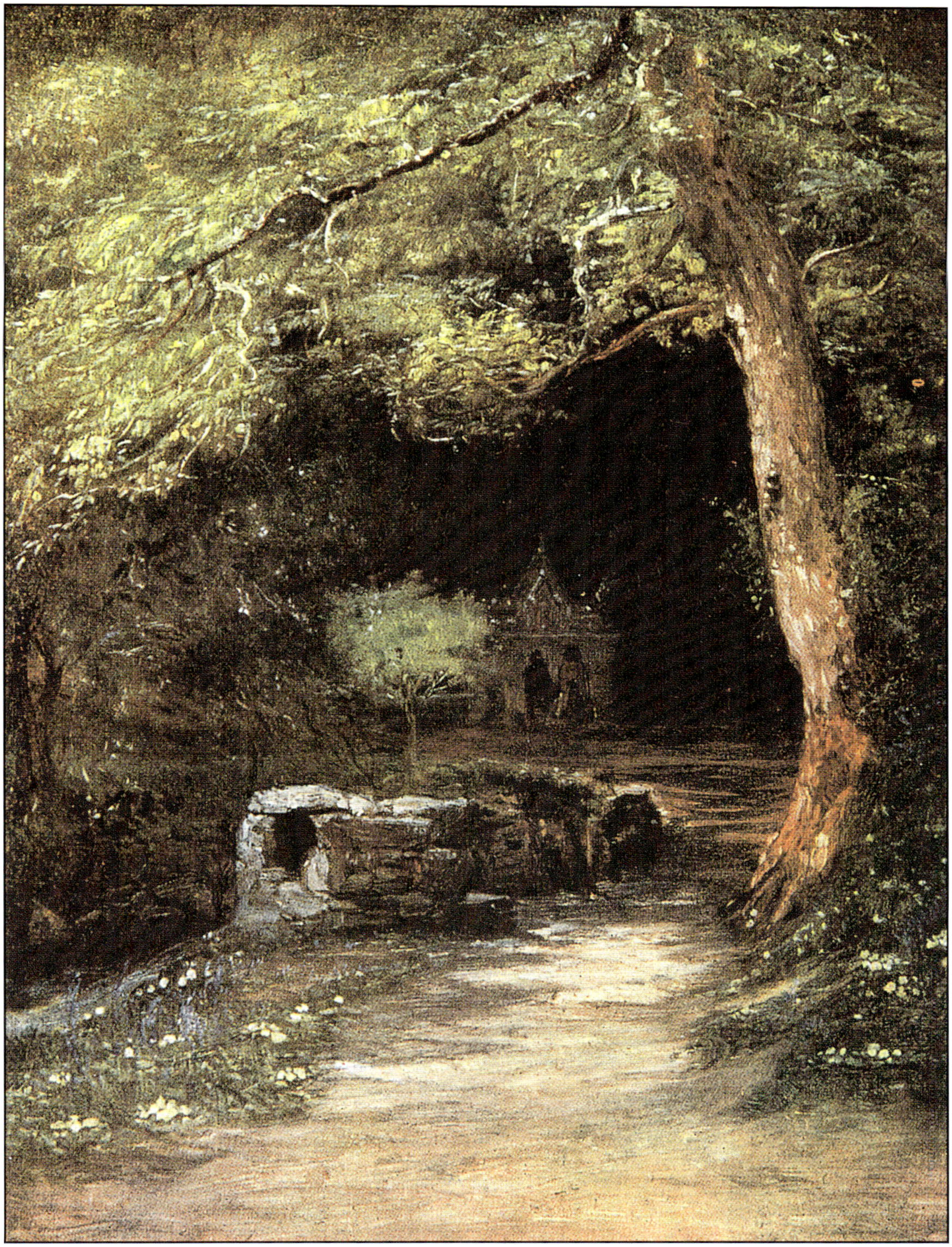

There is no proof that the moat ever existed, but certainly the castles were built and thus the English Pale was defined. With that Henry was content, as were most of the kings who succeeded him until Tudor times. Meanwhile, the descendants of Henry II's knights became Irish, adding a difficulty the king had not foreseen – although he and his descendants might subject the Pale to English rule, they could never make it English.

We know that around 1500, in the time of Tudor King Henry VII, the Pale was defined by a line starting at Dundalk in the north, south-west to Kells, then south-east to Kilcullen, through Ballymore-Eustace and Tallaght to the sea south of Dublin. All the land within this boundary was open and pleasant, not made dangerous by mountains or bogs or forests. It was a country framed for peace.

Of course, since it was in Ireland, peace was often denied it. The recognition of the Pale was enough to cause many attacks; it was harried by the neighbouring chiefs, O'Connors, O'Mores, O'Carrolls, O'Tooles and O'Byrnes, and by many of the Normans besides, when they had become Irish enough to be at war with the English king's Deputy. In addition, the inmates of the Pale had many little wars of their own: but of all these encounters, scant evidence is left. Today, the Pale is full of the loneliness and stillness of Ireland.

If you go to Tara, famous as the site of the chief palace of primitive days, you will find only a little green hill with not even a ruin upon it, and the odds are that you will hear no sound except the lowing of cattle. Whether the palace was ever magnificent, or owed all its fame to the nostalgic imagination of bards, we shall never know. It has vanished. Go to the banks of the Boyne, and you will see only a calm, weedy river winding among moderate hills. Yet there the fate of the British Isles was decided when the last Stuart king – James II – met William of Orange in 1690. Seek Drogheda, whose garrison was massacred by Cromwell in 1649, and though there are ramparts to testify to its former defence, you will find in it no suggestion of war.

When Cromwell landed in Dublin in 1648, he came not only to wreak

"Refreshment for Man and Beast"

Francis Walker noted that this once common announcement had become rare by the time he recorded this scene.

retribution but also to break Ireland once and for all. Drogheda has become the symbol of the zeal with which he carried out this pitiless task. He stormed the fortress and put all its defenders, some 2500 men, to the sword. But this is only the most notorious example of his severity: to this day you may ask any chance-met native of Leinster or Munster about a ruined castle or church of any period and receive the reply, 'Crummle desthroyed it.' From this you might suppose that he would be remembered with hatred, but this is not always so; many of the legends connected with him describe magnanimous conduct.

Take, for instance, the tale of his dealings with Lord Plunkett in Louth. Plunkett, it is said, had lost his way in the dusk after a battle and, stopping to let his horse drink at a ford, was dimly aware of a rider doing the same on the opposite bank. Being worn out, he at first took no notice of him, but as he gazed down at the water he saw the stranger's shadow and on it the glint of a star. From this he knew that the man opposite was Cromwell and, since he could not reach him, he hurled his sword across at him, wounding him in the face, and then made his escape. Some time afterwards he was captured and brought before Cromwell who, mindful of the injury, said, 'I give you your choice of deaths.'

'Then,' said Plunkett, 'give me back my good sword and set any two of your officers to kill me with theirs.'

At this, Cromwell rewarded his courage by setting him free, on the condition that in each future generation of Plunketts there should be one christened Oliver.

There are many more tales showing this side of Cromwell's character. In others, however, he is credited with a more unpleasant humour. It is told that he intended to spare Jerpoint Abbey from the destruction that accompanied most of his journeying through Ireland, but as he marched past it, he heard the abbey bells peal out in celebration as soon as he was out of sight. He therefore returned and destroyed it, saying jocosely that it proved the folly of rejoicing too soon.

The truth is that the Irish have always revered fortitude, and this is the quality

ROSSTREVOR

Situated on the inner corner of Carlingford Bay, with a mountainous background, the lower slopes of which are richly wooded to the sea, giving it the appearance of an inland lake. The climate is mild which is why the place is often known as the 'Mentons of Ireland'.

they admired in Cromwell. In Drogheda his name now excites little emotion. The ruins he made are his monument, but nobody heeds them. The thought of that day of havoc is lost in the remembrance of quietude, for even when the city was fortified it was enveloped by the peace of the Pale. As Mathew put it:

> There are many ruins to be seen in the Pale, the hulks of great abbeys such as Mellifont or Monasterboice, and the green wrecks of castles and churches. Some are old and others are recent, but all seem alike: Irish weather has such a way of its own that one cannot discern what has been wrecked for a hundred years and what for a thousand. The abbeys suggest no violent desecration; the castles seem to have suffered a natural decay. You are not impelled to remember the tragedies of outlaws and conquerors: it seems that if there was ever war in the Pale, it must have been a very long time ago.
>
> This impression is felt even in Dublin. You know well enough that the capital of Ireland has seen many agonies; but such associations appear unnatural. The thing you first notice is its depopulated look; its wide streets are so empty and so many of its big houses seem quite deserted that you could imagine that you were visiting a city abandoned by most of its inmates. Nor is this notion transitory, for when you explore outlying streets tenanted by the poorest, you find in them houses that must once have been splendid. Here, you might think, is a city that used to be affluent

Opposite:

CARLINGFORD LOUGH

This sea-arm is land-locked and surrounded by mountains which shelter its shore and make for a mild climate with luxuriant vegetation. The fields and hedges about Warrenpoint, from which Walker made this spring-time sketch, are alive with a feast of flowers and blossoms. The giant Fin MacCoul was said to have made his home on the mountain to the right. According to legend, in a moment of playfulness, he was said to have thrown the 'Clough More' – a granite boulder fifty tons in weight – where it can still be seen, on the hill above Rosstrevor.

and has for some reason declined. You are told not of a tragic past, but of a former wealth.

> Beyond doubt, Dublin was more prosperous once, and more animated, but it was never rich. Tradition has glorified the merry old times when it had a Parliament, and it must be admitted that contemporary letters and newspapers tell of rejoicings then held in those desolate houses; but if you enquire closer, you find how insubstantial those pageants were. Many of them were the insensate displays of a bankrupt magnificence; there were hours when the grey city was lit by the brief splendour of prodigals, but around that illusive light there was poverty; within the sound of those irrational feasts there was starvation.

Another writer, landing in Dublin in 1776, compared the city unfavourably with London:

> Here we see little to cheer or exhilarate reflection, and much to sadden and depress the spirits. Here is indeed a motion; but it is such as is seen when the pulse of life begins to stagnate, or like the wheel of some great machine just after the power which impelled it ceases to act. Here, to be sure, you meet some splendid equipages, and a large suite of lackeys after a sedan chair; you see a variety of houses, and you frequently meet faces fair enough to make Circassia [an area of the Caucasus famed for the beauty of its inhabitants] gaze; but all this scarcely compensates for the painful emotion produced by the general mass.

This traveller met old men who told him how boisterous Irish dissipation had been when they were young, but he saw none of it. He was chilled by the sad and autumnal air of the city. But though he complained of many things, such as the street cries which 'tingle in your ears with all the enraging varieties of the brogue', he soon found himself growing fond of the city – as so many do. Dublin's attraction must be due partly to its wholesome sea air and its

THE BLOODY BRIDGE

This spot is near the base of Slieve Donard, the highest of the Mourne Mountains, almost thirty miles south of Belfast.

delightful surroundings; for it is planted on a most admirable bay and among rising fields behind which olive hills undulate. They first catch your eye when you enter the bay, beginning with the long headland of Howth, then winding inland, coming back to the sea at Killiney, and thence wandering close to it. Mathew remarked that, 'No town was ever more fortunately placed or more constantly dogged by misfortune. You feel this at once: from the first you are aware of Celtic resignation to sorrow.'

The name Dublin means 'the Black Stream', from the darkness of the River Liffey flowing through it, and the city preserved that Celtic title throughout the long control of the Danes (though elsewhere, as in Waterford and Wexford, they left their own names for towns) and the much longer reign of the English. In the heart of the quiet city you come upon a huge solid tower, all that is left of the castle which once loomed over all Ireland. In Queen Elizabeth's time it overshadowed the life of the most distant clans; there was no chief, however remote his country might be, who did not dread it as a probable dungeon and reflect that his head might blacken above it, spiked on its roof. The head of Shane the Proud of Tyrone rotted there, food for the crows. Within the castle walls many were tortured, and even its Deputies were acquainted with suffering: in the space of half a century, four of them – Kildare, Perrot, Essex and Strafford – left the castle to lose their heads in London's Tower. Now the castle's old strength has departed: the wide moat has vanished and so has one of the twin strongholds; the other remains, an obsolete hulk.

Yet the castle saw merry times, too. In the early eighteenth century it was used for lavish balls, as recorded by the socialite Mrs Delany:

> ...on Monday at eight o'clock went to the Castle. The room where the ball was to be held finely adorned with paintings and obelisks, and made as light as a summer's day. I never saw more company in one place; abundance of finery, and indeed many very pretty women. There were two rooms for dancing. The whole apartment of the Castle was open, which consists of several very good rooms;

From the Hill of Howth, Dublin

in one there was a supper ordered after the manner of that at the masquerade, where everybody went at that hour they liked best, and vast profusion of meat and drink, which you may be sure has *gained the hearts* of all guzzlers!

If you are concerned with the past, Mathew wrote, 'you can find in Dublin many old houses linked with desperate rebels or informers…'

…but these remembrances appear as unnatural as those of the castle. Dublin looks as if it were built for pleasure and quietness; indeed, it has a curious resemblance to Paris, though you have to imagine that city fallen and resigned to its fall. This look, and something friendly and homely in its ways, have combined with its surroundings to lend it that peculiar attraction. But when you grow familiar with it, there is a different aspect. If you turn in to St Patrick's Cathedral, you see in its renovated darkness a slab on which is inscribed, in Latin, 'Here lies the body of Jonathan Swift, Dean of this Church, where savage indignation can no longer lacerate his heart.' Swift was a man of the Pale, born in this city, living for a long time outside it at Laracor, and spending in it his last miserable years. Though his indignation had other fuel besides the sorrows of Ireland, these made his heart burn. Those last words of his may remind you that Dublin has always been a city of pain. There is some shadow over it. In its indifferent peace there is something sepulchral. So there is in the strange calm that broods over all the realm of the Pale.

THE SALMON LEAP

This is one of the most beautiful points on the river Liffey, about 12 miles above Dublin. From there the river flows through miles of luxuriant woodlands.

CONNAUGHT

Opposite the English Pale lay the Irish one, the province of Connaught. When Cromwell had broken Ireland he reversed the old policy and, instead of retaining a part for the English, left one for the Irish. In 1652 the Puritans announced that it was 'not their intention to extirpate the whole nation' and the following year they proved this by enacting that its survivors should be permitted to live between the Atlantic and the Shannon. That river formed a natural moat along nearly all the inner side of Connaught; and this divide between Irish and English was strengthened by giving a belt of land next to it to veteran soldiers. Since the land enclosed by the Shannon was especially unfit to be cultivated, there was reason to hope that most of those who dwelt in this prison would soon be quiet. This Irish Reservation was afterwards decreased, as the counties of Leitrim and Sligo were taken from it and also given to the veterans, but as the latter did not appreciate this new gift, the land, like Donegal, was left for the most part in the hands of the natives.

Cromwell's plan of depositing all the Irish behind the Shannon was not carried out with the thoroughness one might have expected from such a man. If anyone could prove that during the whole war he had been 'actively constant' to the English Commonwealth, he was exempted from transportation, as were all working farmers who had not carried arms. Such exemptions should have been few; but they made it possible for bribery and influence to be brought to bear, and thus some of the Irish remained in their homes. Others, in the fullness of time, presumed to break out of the Pale and return. As for the new English settlers, like generations before them they became Irish, so the plan succeeded only in causing a great deal of affliction.

Hospitality

Francis Walker was appreciative of the famed Irish hospitality, saying that it was often 'amongst the poor that this feature of the national character is to be found in perfection; often in the humble cabin one learns to understand the full meaning of an Irish welcome'.

The Irish Pale was an appropriate contrast to the English one. The gaunt moors of Clare, the stark mountains, sedgy glens and wild bays of Connemara, the windy hills and valleys about them have a tragic look. You feel they could never have been prosperous; and they never were, for Connaught has always been full of battles and sorrows.

It is true, though, that it once contained a prosperous city. In 1656 the Commissioners of Ireland alleged that, except London, there was no port in the British Islands more considerable than Galway; and though it is possible that this was not entirely accurate, since they were trying to sell forfeited houses, there must have been justification for the statement. But Galway was Norman and English and Spanish while it was wealthy; it was aloof from Connaught. From 1232, when it was built by Richard de Burgo, it was an isolated fortress controlled by families of Norman or English descent, known as the Tribes. The names of these are Irish enough now, but in those days the men who bore them were classed among the English of Ireland. While these rich merchants had little affection for the English of England, they were proudly apart from the Old Irish, 'the Os and the Macs'. That was why the Corporation of Galway decreed that the Os and the Macs should not be permitted to swagger in the streets. It is recorded that over one of their gates they had an inscription 'From the Ferocious O'Flaherties, Good Lord Deliver Us'.

The City of the Tribes trafficked with Spain, and that gave it a Spanish air. As Mathew noted:

Opposite:

EMIGRANTS

Francis Walker recorded his impressions of the platform of Killarney Railway Station, saying that it was usually crowded by visitors of every nationality, but that when he entered it that day, he found it crowded with those who were about to leave Ireland for ever: emigrants bound for the far west of America. 'Some were cheery,' remarked Walker, 'others excited, a very few silent. Among the latter was an old couple seeing off their daughter whose trunk was labelled "Boston". They kept up bravely until the train began to move, and only then broke down'.

You will see in that silent and desolate place many old houses that will remind you of the stately abodes of Spanish grandees; but in Cromwell's time these were already impoverished, for Queen Elizabeth's long struggle with Spain ruined Galway. By that time the Tribes had for the most part forsaken commerce and were to be found up in the mountains. There they shared the ill luck of Connaught, as the MacWilliams had done before. While Galway flourished apart, few were more detested by it than the MacWilliams, who sprang from the same stock as the Burkes, tracing their descent from the conquering house of De Burgo. They were in Mayo and Connemara and the hills behind Galway, and ranked with the Celtic stocks – the O'Flaherties who reigned by Lough Corrib, and the O'Briens of Thomond, and the sea-roving O'Malleys of Renvyle and the Islands. Now the MacWilliams are fallen and the O'Flaherties are ferocious no more.

The Highlands of Connemara were been held by the Galway Tribes and linked with such names as Martin, Blake, Morris, French, Burke, Bodkin and D'Arcy. From these families sprang the most typical gentlemen of Ireland, the most reckless, the most gallant, the proudest. Here they lived free, for, as they said, the king's writ did not run in Connemara; here they observed the one set of laws respected in Ireland in the merry old times, the Galway Code of the Duel Great hunters and fighters and drinkers, they rejoiced till the inevitable day of reckoning. But the gloom of Connemara – the darkness they loved because it heightened their defiant hilarity – overcame them at last. Ballinahinch, the palace of the Martins, has long been silent, and by the end of the nineteenth century Renvyle of the Blakes had become a hotel.

In the heart of the mountains, beyond the Pass of Kylemore, a low, wandering, panelled house sits beside the Atlantic; this is Renvyle, and it is worth notice because it is a type. In the old days, while some prodigals built themselves castellated palaces, wiser men who preferred to spend their money on horses and claret, or to run into debt for them, had a modest way of

The Quay, Galway

Many buildings in Galway bore witness to the town's old trading associations
with Spain. On the quay, the houses, although belonging to a more
recent past, still seemed 'foreign-looking'
to Francis Walker.

adding a wing to their houses whenever they thought one was required. From this resulted singular homes, many of them only one storey high, covering a great deal of ground. As Mathew pointed out, these had many advantages:

> ...it was possible for the ladies to sleep undisturbed at one end of them, no matter how joyous the men were at the other; there were no stairs down which a man would be apt to fall in the morning; and the long narrow corridors were convenient for those who found it hard to direct their steps at the end of an evening.

What became of the Irish Nation, beyond the Pale of the Shannon? Where are the descendants of all the families wrecked by that decree of Cromwell's, and herded to live among these rocks if they could? Many of them had been rich, and were given proportionate tracts of wilderness, instead of the pastures of which they were deprived. There were lords among them, and the heads of many of the chief families of the English of Ireland. The decree affected all Royalists (that is, all who were opposed to the Commonwealth Cromwell founded after Charles I had lost his head), be they Protestant or Catholic, rich or poor – except the labourers, who were permitted to stay in their cabins because the new owners would need their service. And they were all sent to particular places: Connaught was divided among the folk of the other provinces. The Burren, for instance, was assigned to the exiles from Kerry, Roscommon to those from Kildare, Meath, Queen's County and Dublin; while Connemara and Mayo were given to those from the North.

All this should make it easy to trace them; and one would expect to find their names prominent still in their compulsory homes. But very few of the landlords of Connaught are today derived from them. It is perhaps not surprising that they failed to retain the Highlands, for in that part they were forestalled by the Tribes, and they could not rest there – Connemara was abhorrent to them. One needs to be happy before one can enjoy that outer gloom. But in the other parts they found lands which were not so unlike those they had lost. So why have they vanished?

Killery Bay – the only Fjord in Ireland

The answer is a complex one. First, they came here as exiles and did not take root in a soil they detested, for in their eyes this was a place of punishment. Nor were they welcome in it, for its original stock, though pitying them, could not but resent their intrusion. That is why the fishermen of the Chaddagh call anyone who intrudes in their midst 'a transplanter'. Many left Ireland for ever when they could, becoming soldiers of fortune in Austria, Spain or France; the rest vanished from prominence because they were beggared. You will find their descendants not among the landlords, but under the thatched roofs of the cabins.

As Mathew observed, this may help to account for the character of the poor in these parts:

> The peasants of Galway are melancholy people. Talk with any fisherman or ragged labourer, or any obstinate man trying to induce his potatoes to grow on a rock, and you will discern it. You will discern also an irrational pride and a grave courtesy. A like lordliness prevails in the similar Highlands of Scotland, and you might infer from this that it is primeval and perhaps caught from the mountains. But if you did so you would fail to appreciate the especial quality of the sad pride you find here. It tells of the memory of lost rank. You will discern other things – for instance, an absolute ignoring of laws, not in a rebellious spirit, but in an oblivious one, such as is natural to men who have suffered much with enforced patience at the hands of a usurper. With such a spirit the transplanted must have toiled in the rocks – quite broken, but never acknowledging Cromwell. You will find also that these men think little of the present and dream of an impossible past or future. It was by this means that the transplanted were able to live.

> In other parts of Connaught the character is different. The men of Clare are a strong, stalwart brood. No doubt they have been hardened by the keen air of their storm-beaten moors. They are always on their guard, slow to make friends, quick to take

A Mountain Dwelling

The occupant of this isolated house told Francis Walker how every morsel of food or anything necessary had to be carried up on the back of man or beast. "There never was a doctor at my door," the poor woman told Walker, "and I have thirteen children".

umbrage; they have the look of men accustomed to watch for enemies and able to see them a long way off. But if you can win their hearts, their friendship is true. In Mayo the people are mild, often dejected, and very prone to self-pity. There the remembrance of misfortune is crushing. They lack the particular pride of sad Connemara and the embittered independence of Clare; they have borne too many blows in more recent times, for many of them are sprung from those driven with violence from the Protestant North.

Such distinctions of character are to be seen in each county of Connaught; but there is one thing common to all, and that is resentment. Much more than in any other province of Ireland, there is in the Irish Pale an abiding sense of injustice. That is the one fruit of Cromwell's plan.

There is one thing to be said in defence of Cromwell's action: he herded his victims into a beautiful prison. But it is fair to conclude that he did not intend to alleviate their punishment in this way, for he never marched here, and it is not likely that he would have admired Connaught in any case. But, whether Cromwell knew it or not, there is an infinite charm in this country of sorrow. Though it was not there for the transplanted, their children have found it. It is most evident in dark Connemara, the Land of the Bays of the Sea. Connemara is a country of shadows: on the bright days they drift on the waters, for the tarns and the inlets are all under hills, and they roam on the mountains when the weather is dark. To love it, you must first understand the pleasure of pain. And if you love it, you will think of it always as dark; you will remember not the brief sunshine but the days when the mountains seemed to exult in defiance or to glory in suffering. All the wild country beyond the wild Shannon seems lulled in an unnatural sleep on days when the wind is still and the sun is out. But when the storms rave in the mountains, then the West is awake.

NEAR RECESS, CONNEMARA

'After leaving Galway westward,' Francis Walker recorded, 'we get the first impression of Connemara on approaching Recess; here the Twelve Pins, or Bens, standing clear and bare, without a vestige of foliage, dominate the landscape in all directions. They arise from what is practically a great plain through which run rapid streams, while close under the hills are several loughs that suggest a fisherman's paradise'.

SOUTH FROM DUBLIN

Cromwell was not content with enclosing the Irish; he determined that the whole seaboard of St George's Channel should be especially garrisoned. Of the coastline facing Scotland and England, Antrim and Down were held by the Presbyterian settlers, and the English Pale had long been subjected, but he felt that the counties south of Dublin required his attention. In the old days the watchmen aloft on Dublin Castle had seen a hostile country whenever their eyes were turned to the South, for the grey hills of Wicklow had always been retained by the Irish. That was the country of the warlike O'Tooles.

This state of affairs had been in part remedied before Cromwell arrived, since the O'Tooles had been broken at last, and he had done something towards ending it when, after his triumph at Drogheda, he had marched ravaging from Dublin to Wexford. Still, he considered that there was room for improvement; so in July 1654 he enacted that all Papists, rich or poor, should disappear from the counties of Wicklow, Wexford, Carlow and Kildare, and from the parts of Dublin below the Liffey, and that any who disobeyed should be court-martialled and executed as spies.

This part of Ireland, which was thus to become thoroughly Protestant, was bounded by the Liffey to the North and the Barrow to the West, and was known as the Five Counties. Two of these counties, Carlow and Kildare, were inland, but they adjoined the others and were fertile, as indeed the

DELPHI LOUGH

This lough which is said to resemble the Greek valley of the same name, is
surrounded by lofty mountains, averaging 2500 feet high, and is
on the road which runs from Killery to Lough Doo and Louisburgh,
and lies in one of the most impressive passes
in Connemara.

whole district was, for even in Wicklow there were rich valleys among the hills. Here no one was to be allowed to employ a Catholic in any capacity, nor to tolerate the sight of one.

This resolute scheme succeeded only in part. The new landlords found it impossible to secure enough Protestant menials and labourers; and many of those who were imported from England fell into Irish ways. The result was that while nearly all the mansions belonged to Protestants, most of the thatched roofs sheltered Catholics. Another result was that these Catholics, like the poor of the Irish Pale, had for some time a vivid remembrance of wrongs. So by attempting to make the Five Counties a Protestant stronghold, Cromwell inspired the ferocity of the Wexford Rising of 1798.

If the men of Connemara had risen, making a last desperate stand in the mountains to which they had been banished, it would have appeared natural enough; but when you see Wexford's soft meadows and gradual moors and wide level roads under branches, and note the methodical and respectable lives of its people, it is hard to believe that this was the scene of Ireland's most frantic rebellion. But there can be little doubt that if the people of Wexford had found a general worthy of the name, and if they had been backed by their fellow-countrymen, they would have succeeded; unhappily for them they had captains who knew nothing of war and they were left to fight their battle alone. So how was it that they succeeded at all, as they did for a time? It could be said that it was because they were among the least Irish of Irishmen.

The county of Wexford has been continually stocked from abroad. The Danes peopled it when they built the town they called Weissfiord at the mouth of the Slaney; the Normans first landed on its southern shore on the Beaches of Bannow and copied the Danes; 'Strongbow', the twelfth-century Earl of Pembroke, colonised it from Wales, and to this day the folk of the baronies of Bargy and Forth have much more in common with their Welsh kinsmen than with their neighbours in Ireland. More English settlers came,

The Gladdagh – A Village on the Opposite Side of Galway Harbour

then the Cromwellian flood, and afterwards Dutchmen. And through all the time, and probably from prehistoric days, there was a steady communion with Cornwall and Wales. Just as Antrim was always in touch with Scotland, so was Wexford with the more southerly Celts on the other side of the St George's Channel.

From all this it came to pass that the men of Wexford had in their nature a foreign element. As Mathew put it:

> ...because they were law-abiding and dogged, they were more dangerous when they were frenzied; because they had always lived in union, they struck together; and they rose, instead of talking about it and postponing it, because they were silent and not given to dreams.

In those days there must have been in this country a look of what Mathew called 'Dutch primness'. There were a great many windmills on the wide moors, and plenty of solid farms in the meadows. But in that terrible year of 1798 most of those farms were wrecked, and from that day on few of the windmills have signalled to one another – many gaunt deserted towers stand in their place. One such tower, or rather the butt of it, stands on a green shoulder of the moors above ripe pleasant fields. From its narrow door you look down on quiet Enniscorthy, a cluster of old houses beside a weedy and shaded little river. The green side beneath the ruin is called Vinegar Hill. In that roofless butt the rebels imprisoned their victims; on that long slope they encamped, or rather huddled, with the sky as their roof, and made their last stand when all hope was gone.

The rebels comprised men, women and children of all ages; for when once that death-struggle had begun, the most peaceful and the most timid alike fled to the camps out of fear of the yeomen. These yeomen were Irish, and so were the militia and nearly all the troops fighting for England, except the German mercenaries. And they all wreaked vengeance with a Puritan rage. It

WILD RHODODENDRONS, CONNEMARA

was a national affair, and each side showed Irish courage and Irish cruelty. It was an internecine religious war in which each side was desperate, and not without reason.

So how was it that Wexford struggled and fell alone? This was in part caused by its habitual independence. The word had gone round to every village in Ireland; but at the last moment the day of the general rising had been postponed. It may be that the leaders from other parts of Ireland had not counted much on the quiet men of Wexford, so did not trouble to warn them of the change; or perhaps Wexford knew of it and chose not to take heed. Because its people were slow to make up their minds, they were the less likely to alter them. Besides, you must remember the disparateness of Ireland. Each county was aloof, as the Swiss cantons and even the English shires once were, and they could only have been united by following some common leader. The men who became Wexford's leaders were quite unknown outside the county. For all of these reasons it came to pass that while the Battle of New Ross was raging on one shore of the River Barrow, the peasants of Kilkenny were to be seen digging and ploughing on the other.

New Ross had been in its time typical of Wexford, for its first fortifications were built to exclude what the historian Holinshed described as its 'naughtie and prowlying neighbours'. This battle, its last, was typical, too, of the ways not only of the county but also of all Ireland, for when it was begun by mistake a great many of the rebels abandoned both hope and their comrades. In the same way the other counties of Ireland, despairing before there was any need to despair, left the men of Antrim and Wexford without help. It is worth noting that the only struggles in 1798 were in Protestant Antrim and in Cromwell's Five Counties.

Of these five the most frequented is Wicklow. This is due to its position near Dublin and to the fact that its charms have been made familiar in song. It is not to be compared with the Highlands of the battered and mournful West – those are of sterner stuff. Here the hills are more pleasant and the smooth

BRAY HEAD, WICKLOW

valleys find a quieter sea. Yet even over placid Wicklow the sorrow of Ireland broods. Cromwell's work was done thoroughly here: there is hardly a ruin to tell of the centuries of Irish defiance. Instead of ivied castles you see Georgian houses, all built to command delectable views. These suggest the enviable lives of retired tradesmen or of families who, drawing their rents from less fortunate places, chose to live here within sight of the Viceroy's court. You may chance to remember other things, strange and true tales of the old chiefs, or incidents of the exterminating war, but of such matters there is no trace, for Cromwell and his men eradicated even the ruins when at length they established in Wicklow the peace of the Pale.

In this sepulchral peace there is the suggestion of sanctity that was recognised when burial grounds were called God's Acres. Wherever you go in Ireland you tread consecrated ground. Here among these mellow hills and serene valleys you find that the domination of the primitive monks prevails. It was restored by the English when they made Wicklow a solitude again. The castles of the chiefs were obliterated; but the rude huts and chapels that were so ancient in their time have survived. Visit Glendalough, that dim hidden lake, of which it is told that some spell forbade any bird to sing above it, and you will find it so mysteriously lulled and so separate that you could not imagine that it had ever been profaned. It seems dedicated still to the men who in this refuge forgot transitory cares.

LISMORE CASTLE

The castle occupies a fine spot on the banks of the Blackwater and was built on the site of the ancient College of Lismore which was said to be a place of great learning, numbering Alfred the Great among its scholars. There are no architectural remains of the College, but a crozier found built into the wall of the castle and thought to be nearly 900 years old, compares favourably with some of the best specimens of Celtic art.

SOUTH-EAST
AND SOUTH-WEST

One of Cromwell's Five Counties, Kildare, had long been held by a branch of the descendants of Maurice Fitzgerald, known as the Geraldines. Fitzgerald, one of the first Norman knights to cross over from England, had also once controlled Wexford, but this had passed under the influence of another Norman line, the Butlers of Ormonde, so named for their ancestor Theobald FitzWalter Le Boteler. Cromwell was not greatly concerned with the Geraldines, for the branch of the family that held Kildare had been broken by Henry VIII and made loyal to England; the other, the Fitzgeralds of Desmond, had been almost annihilated in Elizabeth's reign. But he had much to do with the Butlers, for the Marquis of Ormonde commanded the Irish Nation. For hundreds of years these two families had been lords of the South: Munster was divided between them. It was lucky for England that they had been rivals, hating one another and struggling for mastery, else they would indeed have been a powerful force for resistance.

Beginning to rise at the same time, in the early fourteenth century, when a Fitzgerald was made first Earl of Kildare and a Butler first East of Carrick, these two great Norman houses flourished while greater ones fell; they were expanding their realms long after the Heritage of the Earl Marshall and the Earldom of Ulster, once much more potent titles, were things of the past.

At first the Geraldines prevailed in the long struggle between them, owing to the fact that Kildare was near Dublin and their other strongholds were separate and out of reach of the Deputies. Then the Butlers gained an

MYRTLE GROVE

This is Sir Walter Raleigh's house where he entertained Edmund Spenser. The first Irish potatoes were grown in the adjoining garden.

advantage, for the marriage of a daughter of their house to Thomas Boleyn, though at first involving them in trouble, later gave them influence and made them Queen Elizabeth's kinsmen.

For generations the two houses filled the annals of Munster with their interwoven tragedies. Where could you find a tale more romantic? On the Geraldine side, the eighth Lord Kildare was made Deputy by Henry VII because none could control him.

'All Ireland cannot rule this earl?' had asked the king. 'Then let this earl rule all Ireland.'

The ninth Lord Kildare, also a Deputy, was cast into the Tower by Henry VIII and sent from it a silken heart and black dice to his son, known ever afterwards as Silken Thomas, who was ruling in his stead. Thomas, taking these tokens as an appeal for vengeance, rode to Dublin Castle, flung down his sword of state on the Council table and plunged into rebellion, thus dooming himself and four of his uncles to die on the gallows.

The history of the Butlers of Ormonde contains many equally dramatic tales. The provinces of Leinster and Munster were for many a year greatly concerned with both of these houses; and each has left a mark on them still.

Opposite:

St Mary's, Youghal

This church was originally a Franciscan abbey, founded in the thirteenth century.
Francis Walker's picture shows the font, screen and carved oak pulpit
which he found remarkable for their ancient craftsmanship.
He observed that the part of the church in which they stood
appeared to be completely original,
unlike the rest of the church which had
been heavily restored.

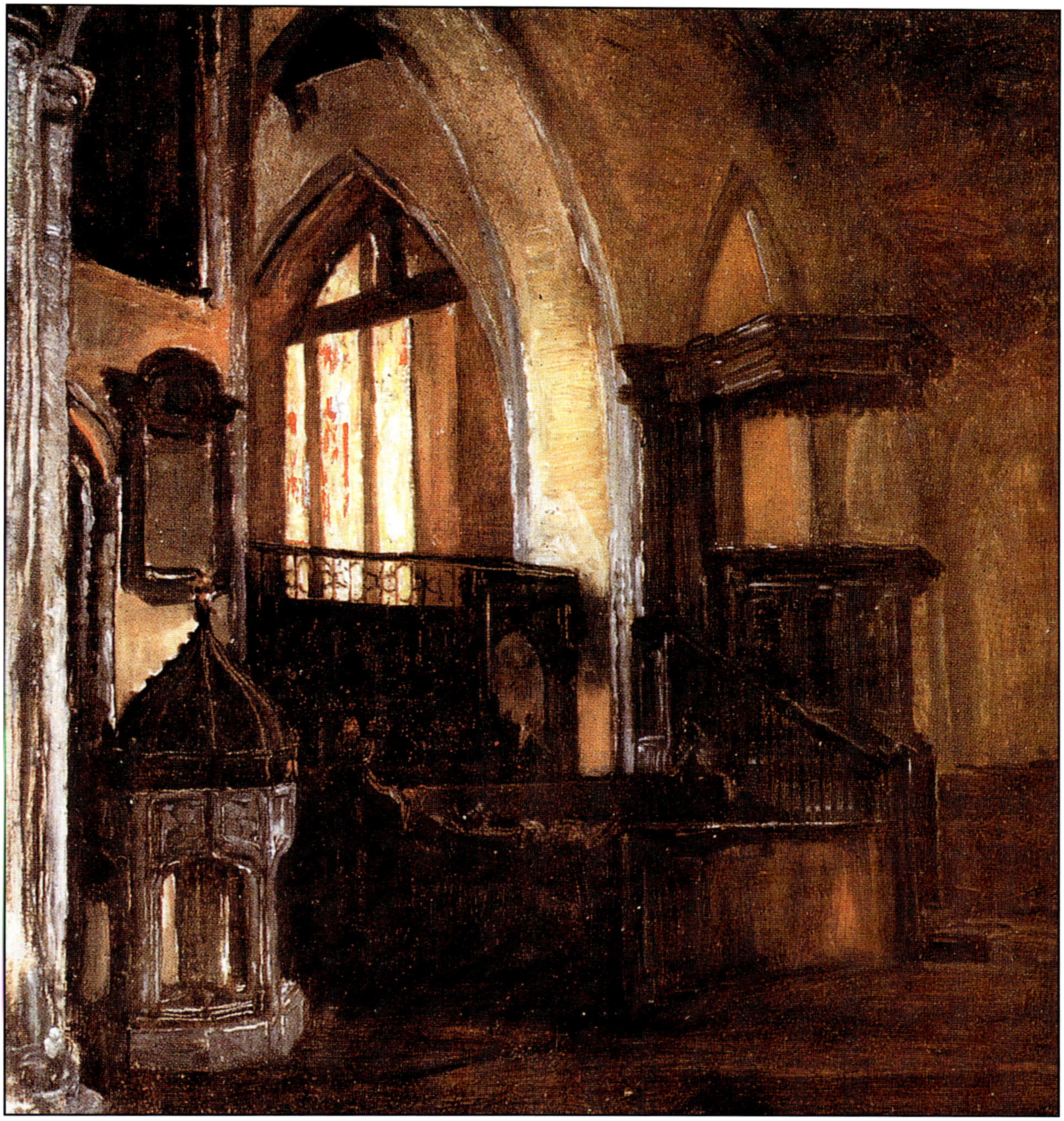

The fortunes of war gave the Geraldines a place in the affections of Ireland never gained by the Butlers. The vanquished cause is dear to the Irish, and it so happened that the Geraldines of Kildare and of Desmond went down in rebellion (one branch to rise again, the other to be mighty no more) and thus won the name of patriots. In addition to this it was remembered that they had always been reckless and pious and open-handed and loving, none of which qualities were shown by their rivals.

Frank Mathew described the fortunes of the Butlers thus:

> Kilkenny became the chief hold of the Butlers, for though in the course of time they recaptured Tipperary, in one way or another it was never so thoroughly theirs. Kilkenny Castle seems to denote their stable good fortune; it has a look of immemorial security; and the city it dominates, Kilkenny of the Steeples, appears as fortunate. Indeed, you could imagine that the whole county had shared the same exceptional luck. It will seem vacant, if you compare it to an English shire, and its green valleys have Ireland's strange quietness, like the peace of a land recently swept by some terrible storm; but it will not suggest misery. It is orderly because it is prosperous.
>
> In all this there is something deceptive. Most of that ivied castle is modern, and its ancient portion endured conquering sieges; that ecclesiastical city was sacked by Cromwell; and the folk of those

Opposite:

MOUNT MELLERAY

The monastery was founded in 1830 by Cistercian monks expelled from France. Having been granted a tract of wild mountain land by the late Sir Richard Keane of Cappoquin, they built this monastery and transformed the brown stony waste into a well-wooded, cultivated haven which supplied all their material wants.

valleys had more than their share of war. As for the Butlers, though they thrive now, it is after many vicissitudes. Yet they had an obstinate knack of surviving misfortune and retaining their grip, and that kept the county Norman. If you will not find many Norman names in it, that is because most of the knights and their followers took Irish ones after a time. But the people have the pride, the activity and the shrewdness of the Normans; though they have adopted an Irish side, too, in that for hundreds of years they have been both very quarrelsome and very religious. They have fought much and suffered greatly; but they have been permanent, and they have owed this to the Butlers; for when the Royalist first Duke of Ormonde came home from exile in France after the defeat of Charles I, he made short work of the Cromwellian intruders.

A native of Tipperary, Mathew continued his narrative in this way:

It was not so on the neighbouring moors of Tipperary. This county, the heart of Ireland and, some say, the most excellently Irish of all, has attracted adventurers time after time; but it has made them its own. It was always a place of battles and its appearance is martial. The bold moors bred fighters, and the rich fields were the spoils of the strong.

There are few traces now of the primitive wars or the original Kings of Thomond and Munster: most of these are obliterated, and though you find only too many ruins, most of them tell of later strife. One indeed is a link with a more remote past: this is Cashel, the cathedral that stands high on a solitary rock. Cormac MacCullinane, king and archbishop and saint, began

Opposite:

THE MONKS OF MOUNT MELLERAY

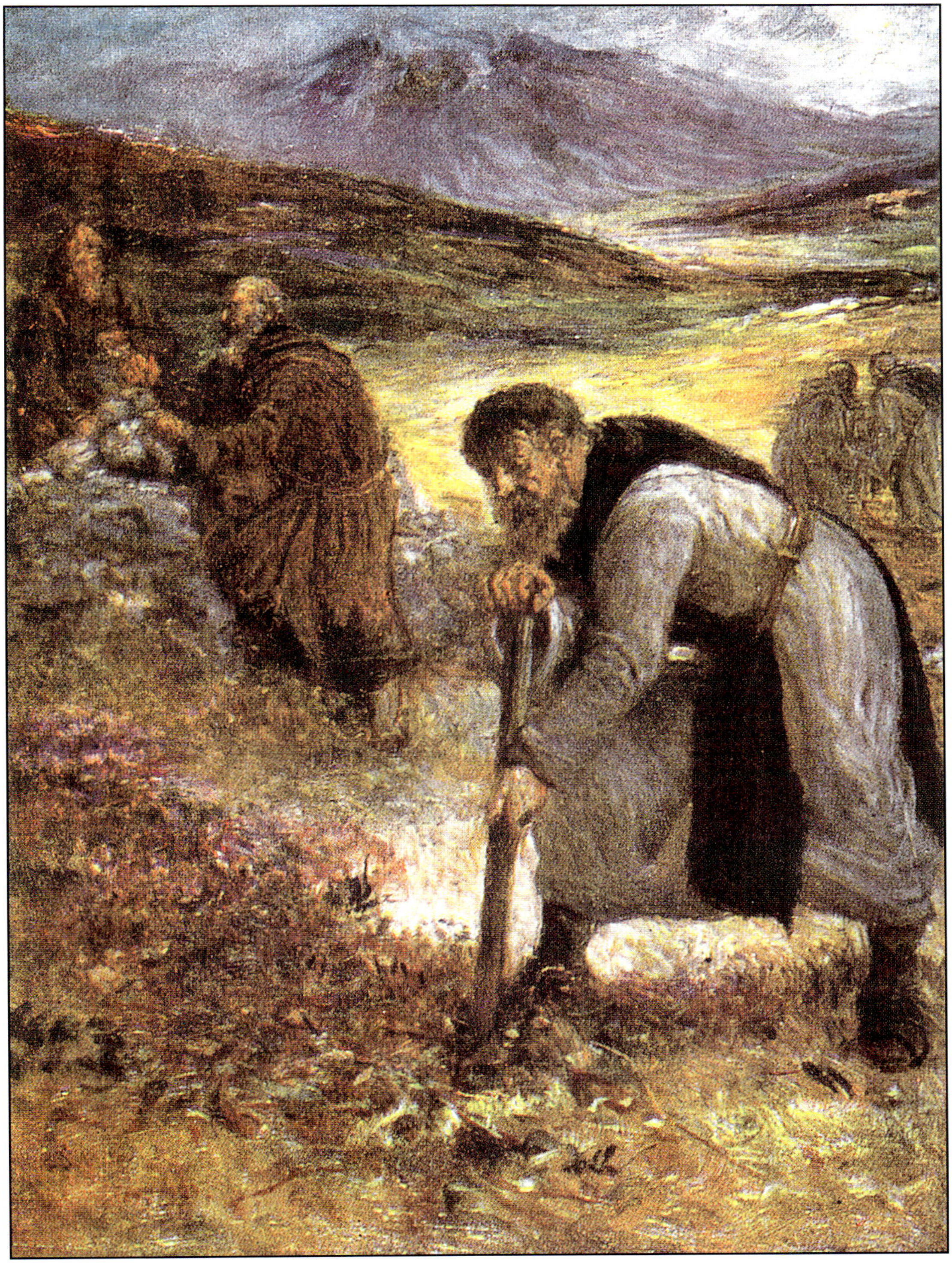

it in 827, though the chapel ascribed to him was built long afterwards by Cormac MacCarthy. The eighth Earl of Kildare burnt it – which outrage he excused by alleging that he had supposed that the Archbishop of Cashel to be inside at the time – and Lord Inchiquin, 'the Wavering Panther', sprang on it with his Puritans, stormed it through one of its painted windows and filled its aisles with dead. So ended Cashel of the Kings.

Holy Cross Abbey, too, dates from the times before the Normans arrived. But almost every other ruin indicates Norman magnificence and the wars between the Butlers and the Geraldines, or the havoc wrought by Cromwell. The latter, in fact, had no need to strike terror here, for he had done it sufficiently at Wexford and Drogheda, and few had the courage to brave his blood-stained sword. Several of the strong castles surrendered without striking a blow. Clonmel alone fought to the last, and in its case the garrison were men from the North under Black Hugh O'Neill. The South had lost heart, persuaded that resistance was in vain.

After this no part of Ireland was more thoroughly cleared of its former proprietors. In time a few came back from Connaught, and others, who happened to be allied with the Butlers, regained their land; but most of the landlords and farmers were uprooted. The greater part of the county passed to Cromwellians, many of them Puritan officers who had purchased the shares assigned to their soldiers. These officers were short-sighted; for if they had encouraged the veterans to settle there, in accordance with Cromwell's plan, they would not have been forced to permit so many Irish to remain or return. As it was, many of the peasants survived the storm that swept their masters away; but even the children of these often have a foreign strain, and you will find English names under the thatched roofs on the hills. Mathew described the people of his homeland, including some members of his own family, thus:

> These people are a stubborn stock, with a rough pride of their own and a cheerful and bold conviviality. Here you find none of the subjected despondence of a broken race. As for the landowners, Cromwellians or

KINCORA

Francis Walker described this spot and its surroundings as 'perhaps the most beautiful on the Shannon'.

not, of Fighting Tipperary, they were great in their time. They are decimated now and impoverished, but while they multiplied they were second to none in exhibiting the virtues and vices of Ireland.

On these moors or in the meadows below them there are many old houses that were once famous and are now left desolate. Such a one, for instance, is Thomastown Castle. Just as Renvyle was a type of one kind of home, so Thomastown represented another. It was a huge castellated house: its upper storey was crammed with many bedrooms and its other contained spacious and lofty halls. There were gardens beside it, made after the English fashion, full of terraces and hedges – clipped in the likeness of impossible birds – and statues and grottoes; and around it lay an orderly park of 2000 acres. It was dedicated to hospitality, after the Irish fashion. Yet its owners, the Mathews, were but recently Irish, being descended from George Mathew of Llandaff, who married his cousin, Lady Thurles, the first Duke of Ormonde's mother, in 1637. Tipperary had soon conquered them.

Under the roof of Thomastown was born Father Theobald Mathew, the Apostle of Temperance, who worked wonders for Ireland because he loved it so much and understood it so well. Having signed the pledge in 1832, he crusaded all over Ireland,

Opposite:

A WOMAN'S TASK

Francis Walker recorded this scene along the north coast towards Gweedore and The Bloody Foreland. It was normally the women's task to carry the turf and dig the potatoes. He noticed the remarkable absence of men in the region – presumably they were away working in Dublin or on the English mainland, attempting to escape the grinding poverty of these coastal regions.

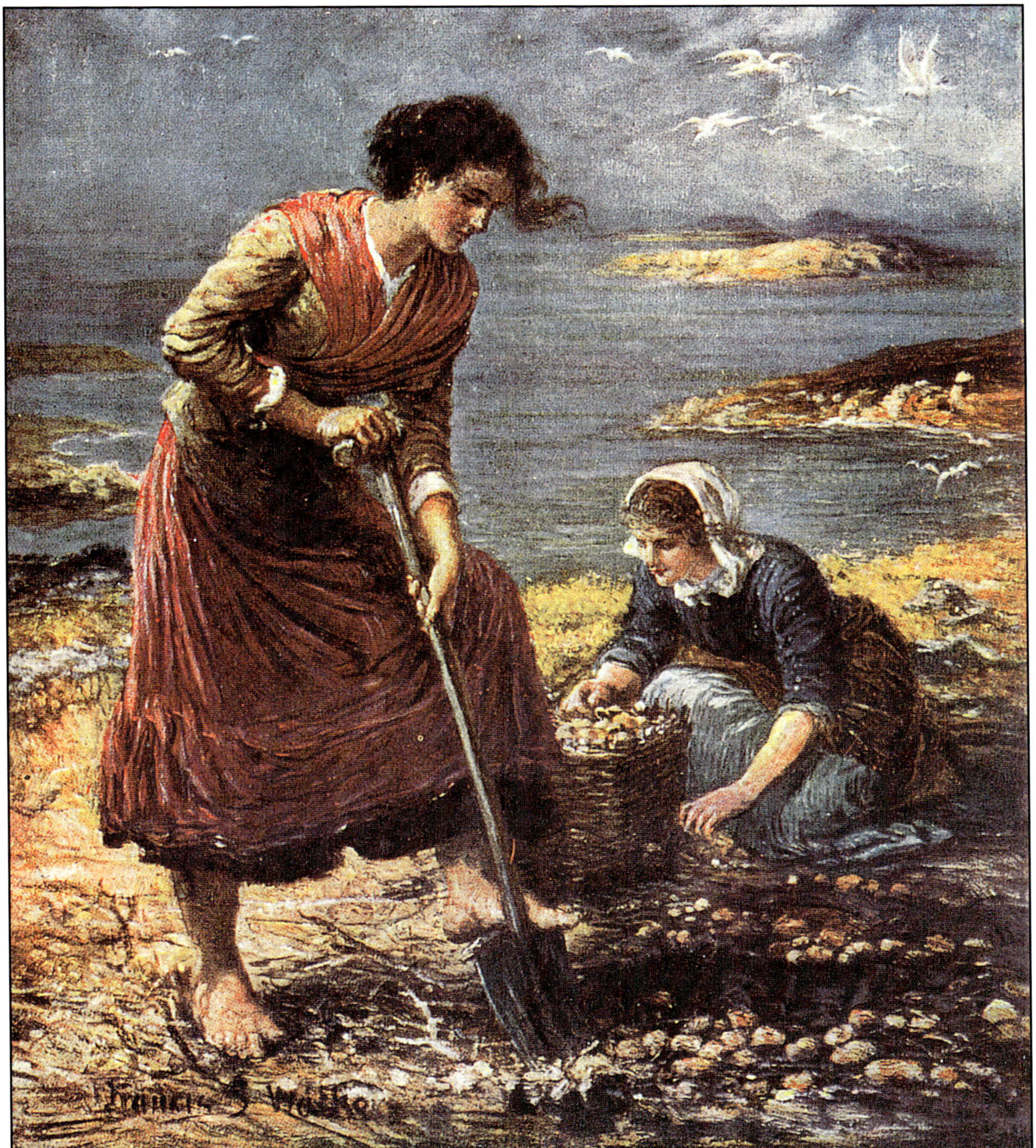

converting men to his gospel of abstinence. He did this not in a churlish and unsocial spirit, but because he earnestly believed it would be of benefit to the poor of his country. When the famine came he worked tirelessly to raise money from England and America to help relieve suffering, and he continued to work tirelessly for many years, until at last his exertions on the part of his fellow Irishmen killed him.

The homes of the Geraldines of Desmond were scattered about the counties of Limerick and Cork and Waterford and the Highlands of Kerry; but in these there were three great independent cities and the realms of other Irish chiefs who, though despoiled of much, clung to their places. It was only in Kildare that the Geraldines were wholly supreme. Their home in that county, Carton, is a modern house, built without any consideration of danger.

There has been a house on the site since the early seventeenth century, but the land on which Carton now stands was forfeited to the Crown in 1691 after the death of the then Duke of Tyr-Connell. He had been attainted for his role adviser to the deposed King James II during the latter's calamitous time in Ireland, and for having fought with him at the Battle of the Boyne. The house was sold at auction and passed out of Geraldine hands for forty years, when the lease was sold back to the nineteenth Earl of Kildare.

It is from this time that most of the house dates. Lord Kildare employed a German architect, Richard Castle, to enlarge and refurbish it, a task he carried out with great skill and enthusiasm, producing as his

Opposite:

Carrying Turf

Two baskets of turf a day kept the fire going, and were carried daily
from the bog to the house, usually by the women of the family.

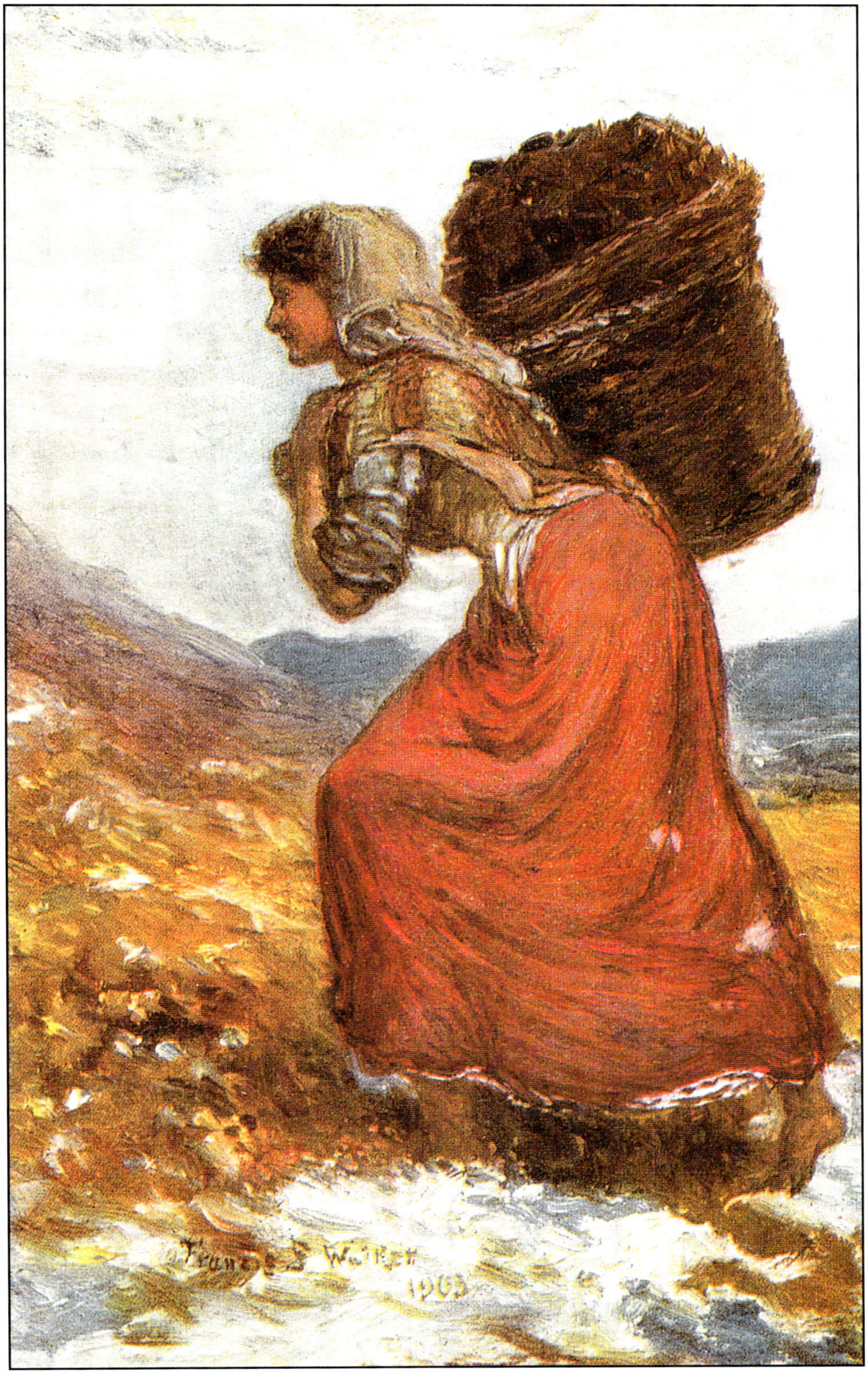

masterpiece a luxurious baroque saloon. Among the adornments to the lavish frieze are to be seen carved monkeys, which also feature in the Kildare coat of arms.

The legend goes that when John Fitz Thomas, later first Earl of Kildare, was an infant, the castle of Woodstock, in which he was living, caught fire. The adults of the household, in their haste to escape, at first forgot the baby, but when at last they returned to the smouldering ruin to search for him, they saw that on one of the surviving towers was an ape, usually kept chained in the castle grounds, carefully cradling the infant in his arms. The Earls of Kildare have, in gratitude, ever since used twin monkeys to support their crest.

The twentieth Earl of Kildare, later first Duke of Leinster, concentrated not on the house but on the grounds of Carton. It is said that he wanted Capability Brown to come to Ireland to oversee the work, but Brown refused on the grounds that he had 'not finished England yet'.

By the river Avon Dhuff, the Black Water, deep in Geraldine country, stands a proud castle, Lismore, fit to be compared with the Butlers' hold at Kilkenny; but it is linked not with the Geraldines but with Sir Walter Raleigh. Lismore had long been the stronghold of monks and an important seat of learning by the time the first castle on the site was built by Prince John, who spent eight months in Ireland in 1185. Once he became king, John seems to have lost interest in this remote corner of his realm, and allowed the

Opposite:

THE PIPER'S VISIT

Travelling musicians or neighbours playing the bagpipes, the flute or fiddle were always welcome in rural Ireland, providing the only diversion in the life of toil led by most villagers. Their arrival meant

a dance which often kept up until
'cock crow in the morning'.

bishops to reside in his castle, with the proviso that the honour should not be accorded to any native Irishman. It was from the bishops that the castle passed to Raleigh in 1589, and although his name is forever associated with it, he owned it for a mere thirteen years. From him it was sold to the Boyles, and from them to the house of Cavendish, and now it is held by the Duke of Devonshire and lords it over a trim little English-style town. The castles in which the Geraldines of Desmond rejoiced are ruins in ivy.

Raleigh profited by the Geraldines' calamity, and if you visit the town of Youghal, in the county of Cork, you will be apt to overlook their traces in seeking his home, Myrtle Grove. Yet that green gabled house is a building of yesterday compared with St Mary's Cathedral, built by the Geraldines long ago. The house and the cathedral ruins stand close together, the former inhabited still and often sought for the sake of the legend that in its gardens tobacco was first smoked in Ireland and the potato first planted; the latter neglected and indeed shunned out of fear of ghosts.

Raleigh was no friend to Ireland – it might even be argued that he was its worst enemy because he introduced the potato – but he is remembered while there is little thought of the race that loved the land so well. Still, you cannot help thinking of the Geraldines when you follow their sad and noble river. You could imagine that the depths of the Black Water were still haunted by the ghosts of the leaves that whispered above it when it ran dark below the forest of Desmond, for it is a wide river of shadows. Beyond doubt it is haunted by the thought of the Geraldines: you remember them at woody Droman and calm Temple Michael and every turn of the riverbank.

Opposite:

THE DARGLE

A wooded glen, a few miles above Bray in County Wicklow

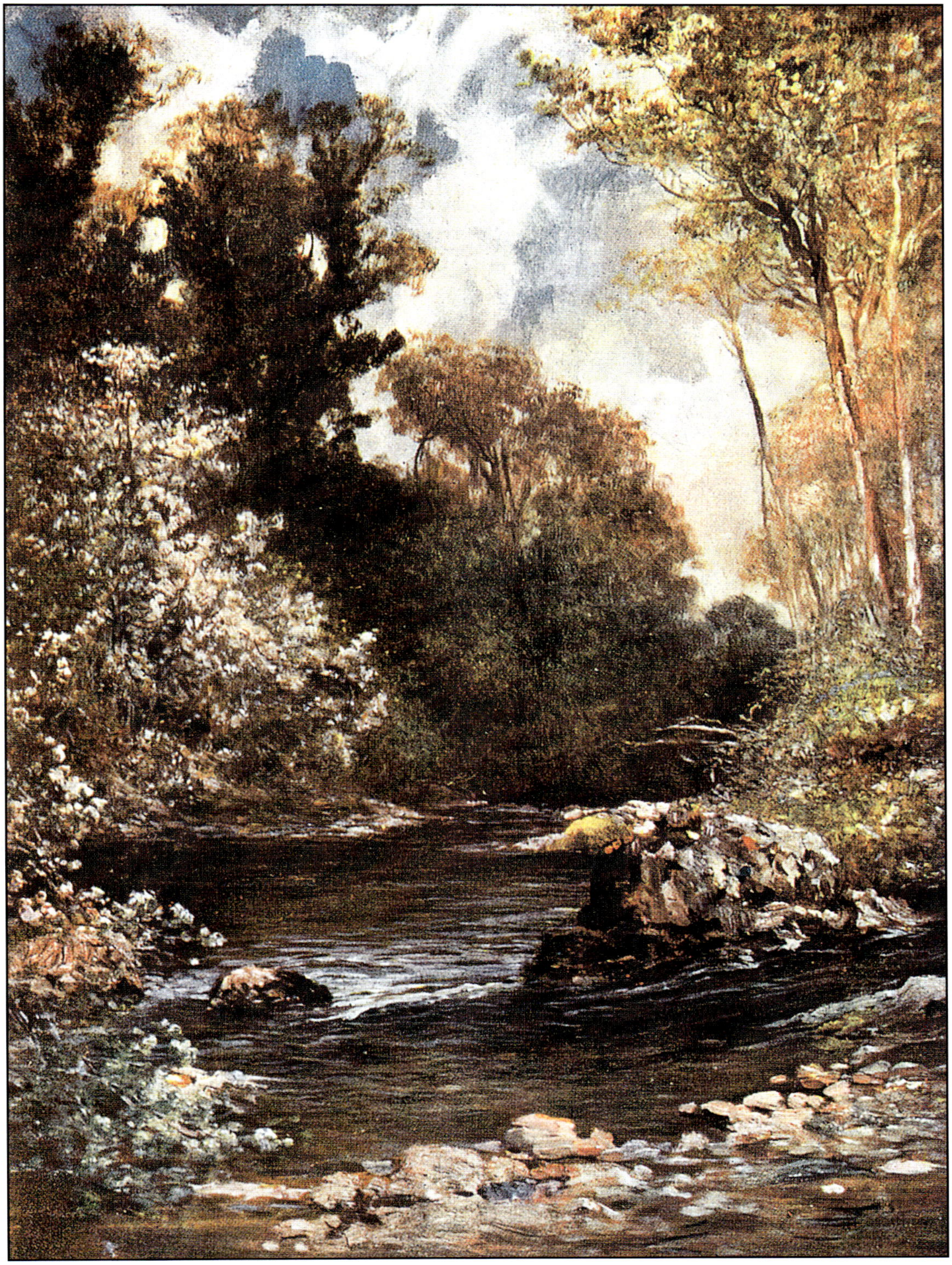

At Temple Michael was their burial place. It is recorded that one of them was buried away from it, at Ardmore on the Waterford side, after fighting in vain. His spirit found no rest there, but haunted the opposite bank at midnight for seven years, calling, 'Ferry Gerald across!' until some faithful clansmen of his brought his body across the river by stealth in the dark.

Another legend has it that in the most ancient times Torna the Druid prophesied that a wind from the south-west would fell the great tree that covered all Ireland. This has been interpreted as a warning that the Fenians would land in the south-west and conquer. Whether they did or not is unknown; whether they even existed is uncertain; what is recorded is that the Danes and Normans came up from the south-east like a devastating wind. That was Ireland's most enticing and vulnerable shore; the Roman Agricola intended to bring his legions there, when, as Governor of Britain in the first century AD, he marched up the Cornish coast and had dreams of expanding his country's empire. So the south-eastern corner of Ireland – the counties of Wexford and Waterford – through attracting many invaders became foreign. The more daring adventurers marched inland; the wiser ones were content to stay where they were.

The Danes founded Waterford City at the head of an inlet that had been called the Haven of the Sun till they came, and was afterwards known as the Glen of Lamentation, because of the mourning that followed the many battles with them. Out of the five cities held by the Danes – Dublin, Cork, Limerick, Wexford and Waterford – this was the one that kept its character most. 'Waterford remains intact' was inscribed on the city's coat of arms, and that motto was always justified. Cromwell besieged it in vain; but it would not admit Royalist troops either. It stood alone, not to be coerced or entangled in the wars of its neighbours.

Opposite:

MARKET DAY

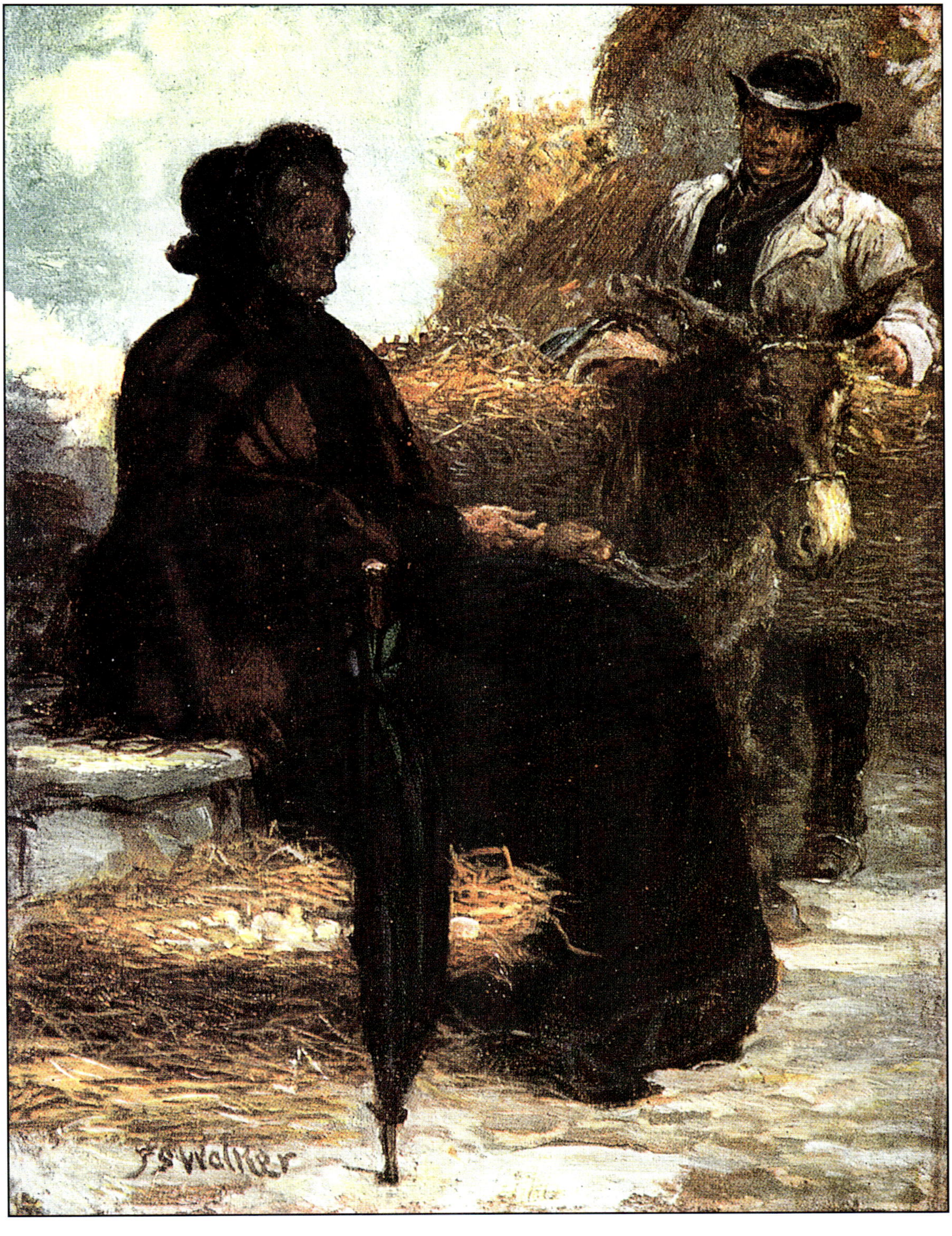
F S Walker

It was not possible for the county to keep as intact as its capital did; yet like Wexford it had a life of its own. Unlike Wexford, it was not thickly populated, and was long held by Norman houses. It was a county fit for stately homes, being well wooded, well watered and fertile; even its mountains will repay cultivation, as was proved by the Trappist monks of Mount Melleray when they turned a bare hillside into rich fields. So the adventurers who found it first kept it as long as they could. For which reason, and because the peasants were as tough and intractable as their neighbours of Wexford, the masterful Geraldines failed on this side of their river. But they were at home in the pleasant county of Cork.

There is a solitary ivied tower standing by a small river, near Buttevant, in a deserted and bare glen. This is all that is left of the splendid Geraldine fortress Kilcolman. When the Geraldines were defeated, it was granted to the poet Edmund Spenser, then serving as secretary to Lord Grey de Wilton, Lord Deputy of Ireland; it came with 3000 acres around it, on condition that Spenser should reside in it and allow no Irish on his lands. Here he wrote *The Faerie Queene*, not without thinking of the Irish and of their knightly deeds in their haunted forest; and here he came under the spell of the glamour of Ireland. More than that, he came under the spell of Irish ill luck, for the castle was burnt in the rising of 1598 and Spenser was driven out of the country, broken-hearted.

Nor were his descendants immune; William Spenser, the poet's grandson, was evicted and transplanted to Connaught as one of the Irish Nation, thus incurring the doom which Edmund had recommended as fit for all the barbarous Irish. Since which time the Spensers have vanished as utterly from ruined Kilcolman as have the Geraldines and the tall woods that once roofed the valley with leaves.

It is probable that the people of County Cork had even then the character recognised now; for it is plain that they attracted their conquerors, and subdued them in turn, not by the sword, but with an irresistible kindliness.

Steeplechasing

This sketch, showing Ireland's national sport, was made at Claremorris, County Mayo.

Even Edmund Spenser – who, when he was not lost in gentle dreams, was evincing a peculiar ferocity towards the Irish which is remembered still by those who were never soothed by his verses – even he married a local girl, and before and after his time many another foreigner came and saw and was conquered.

In Cork on every hand you find tenderness and brightness and 'blarney'. It is related that the word blarney was coined by Queen Elizabeth. The Lord of Blarney Castle, a MacCarthy, so often beguiled her with amiable messages that at length she exclaimed, 'That is all blarney and means nothing.' And, as Mathew put it:

> It must be admitted that if she did say this, she was not far wrong. Cork blarney does not mean very much, beyond a pleasant desire to please: it is best explained by other words popular here, such as wheedling, deludthering, soothering. None of these denotes any culpable guile. The people of Cork hold with St Augustine that an ounce of honey attracts more flies than a gallon of vinegar. Their light-heartedness does not seem to be Irish: you will find it

Opposite:

THE PILLION

In the hilly places of the north and west, where there were very few roads, the pillion was the usual mode of travelling for women. It consisted of a cushion placed on the back of the horse, behind the saddle, on which the woman sat side-ways, holding on to her male companion. Francis Walker was surprised by the pace at which they could go in this somewhat precarious position. It used to be the custom that, following a wedding, the couples who attended the church service would race back in this fashion to the bride's house. The first arrived would welcome the bride and groom and receive special favours during the festivities.

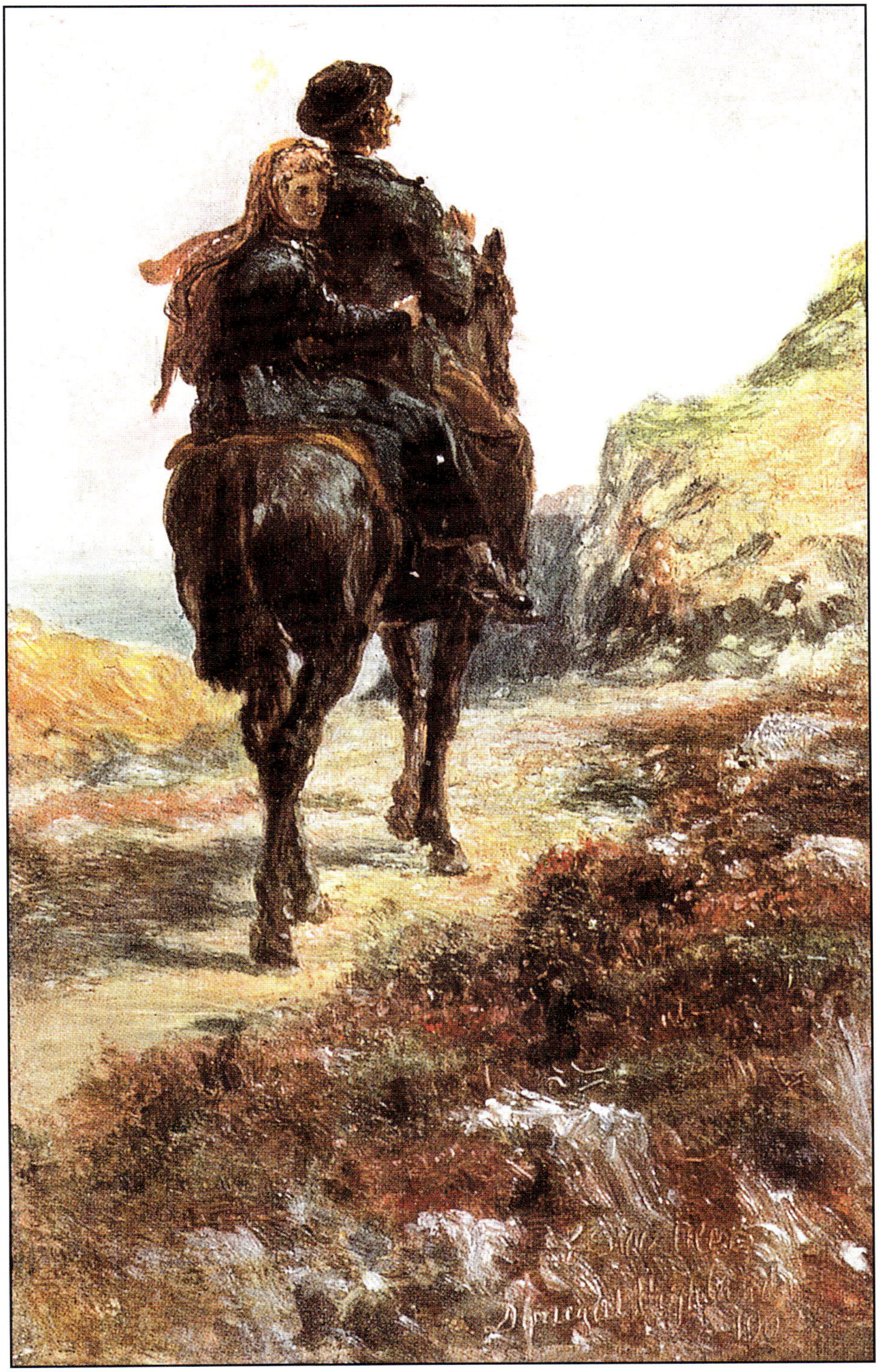

nowhere else in the country, but it seems natural here. The sunny and mild climate of what one writer called the Land of Many Waters, and the soft loveliness of its undulating meadows, accord with the nature ascribed to all who are born within the sound of the Bells of Shandon.

The city earned its name 'Rebel Cork' in the days when it supported Perkin Warbeck, that ill-fated impostor who rose against Henry VII, claiming that he was one of the two royal princes alleged to have been murdered in the Tower, and therefore the rightful King of England. Warbeck was executed in 1499, but Cork remained rebellious. It was an independent city then, its prosperity based on trade, and was always in arms against its 'evil neighbours, the Irish outlaws'. Its long isolation ended almost two centuries later when its ramparts were finally battered by the Duke of Marlborough, the great general in the service of William of Orange.

Frank Mathew described the city in the early years of the twentieth century:

> Cork has no martial look, but rather a happy-go-lucky air of content. Yet if you turn into its by-ways, you will find misery and destitution. When you visit the Cove of Cork, that wide Haven of the Sun, you will be reminded of pleasure by the innocent sails of yachts. But the harbour has also oft been frequented by the emigrant ships which have made it resemble that other Glen of Lamentation: its hilly shores have echoed the loud grief of a multitude. It would have been better for those exiles if they could have looked back for the last time on a scene less delightful; here they could not help but feel how rich and kind a land they were leaving.

Limerick City, until Cork, has retained its martial appearance. There are great solid towers and sheer ramparts; but these are no longer defended, and are as obsolete as the vacant warehouses that tell of a forgotten prosperity:

THE GAP OF DUNLOE

Killarney owes its well deserved reputation as much to the variety
as to the beauty of its scenery.

You feel that this is a place blighted in its prime by some strange misfortune; it is so silent and fallen that you could imagine it under a curse. Yet for a long time it ranked with Galway, it was as proud and as flourishing, and had a much older claim to respect, since it had been famous as a seat of the Danes. Like them, its people were always sea-faring and mercantile and bellicose, till it was broken by its last siege in the days of William of Orange. After that time, it was gradually deserted; its men found their way to the foreign brigades and later to America. Now, though that first impression is modified when you are familiar with the city, though you find that it has more commerce and life than you thought, these appear out of proportion, as when you see a small household living quietly in part of an ancient castle.

Limerick was greatly influenced by the Geraldines, for they were enthroned nearby in Desmond Castle at Adare, on the shore of the lordly and impetuous Shannon. That was a royal house in a royal country: Kincora, the Palace at the Head of the Weir, once stood by the Shannon above it, and so did Castle Connell, the seat of the Kings of Thomond. Now Castle Connell is ruined, and of Kincora nothing is left save a grassy mound. Desmond Castle is a green wreck among the remnants of monasteries that the Geraldines founded. Near all their great homes they built monasteries; it was their boast that they had been the chief patron of the friars and monks. This form of munificence was one of the things that made them congenial.

Limerick County resembles Tipperary and Clare in its boldness; but its moors are more often cloven by valleys. Time was when it was sheltered by the Dark Wood, the forest in which the hunted Irish lay hidden during the fine months, sallying out of it only when the misery of the winter impelled them to a mad desperation – they could not rest under the naked and moaning boughs. Now, though the forest was felled by the conquerors in Elizabeth's time, many of the hollows have grown woody again. And the people of this county have much in common with those of Clare and Tipperary, though they are of more mingled blood. The Germans who were

THE EAGLE'S NEST

This is one of the best known hills in Killarney. Its proximity to the 'Long Range' or river from which it rises perpendicularly makes it a striking sight and appear higher than it really is. Francis Walker observed the grey eagles which nested in its wilderness.

brought to Ireland under Queen Anne took a firmer hold here than anywhere else; beside these there were many Cromwellian settlers, for this was one of the parts kept by the soldiers. So the people have a robust and dogged strain; but their kinship with the natives of Cork has ensured a hilarity that is not to be found in Tipperary or Clare.

When you go westward to the mountains you enter the oldest part of Ireland. The Highlands of Donegal are ancient enough, and so is Connemara, but Kerry belongs to a period of which nothing is known. In Killarney you will remember the monks; but that fortunate place is only an outlying nook of waters and trees and flowers. A dark river, fighting its way along a trough of the mountains on the brink of the Highlands, widens into pools above hollows, and then into a small lake, and next into a larger one, and afterwards is constricted again till it reaches the ocean.

Its two wide and sunlit expanses are now called the Lakes of Killarney. Because it reposes in them, they tell of rest amid toil and forgetfulness amid trouble. Their delicate light is the more welcome because it is contrasted with the gloom of the mountains. The nook has a restful and calm prettiness. This is such a place as a man would choose when abandoning a world he found too hard and seeking oblivion. So it was a favourite haunt of monks, but it does not suggest the grave silence of hermits as Glendalough does; it reminds you of the happiness found in scholarly cloisters and of peaceful and ordered lives. It is true that you will come on the hulk of a castle once held by the O'Donoghues of the Lakes, and will find pleasant spots vulgarised by such names as O'Sullivan's Punchbowl, and if you are foolish enough to allow the boatmen to plague you with stories, most of which have been concocted for English consumption, you will hear many absurd legends of non-existent chiefs and very little about the monks; but if you dwell on these things you will fail to appreciate the charm of the place. You will not feel it unless you are persuaded for a little that all the tragedies and cares of the world are the things of a dream.

Moonlight on Muckross

But this spot, which might be called, as part of it is, the Glen of Good Fortune, is excepted from the mournful and wild Kingdom of Kerry. It is a spot of light in the darkness. Behind its rich woods stand bare heights, and that changing river is darkened by the Gap of Dunloe. If you should ascend that river to its source, you would find yourself under Cruacha Dhu, the Black Reeks, and in the heart of a wilderness where the gloom is primeval. And the people of the Kingdom of Kerry, the few representatives of its desperate clans, have in their nature much that is primitive. If you can get to know them at all (and that is not easy) you will feel that the first wandering men who found their westward course limited on this brink of the world must have resembled them. They have never been understood by their neighbours, and in consequence they have seldom been trusted. Perhaps the distrust arose partly because they were suspicious. So were the primeval men: one can imagine them dark and silent, and gregarious only because they were afraid.

This is a land less shadowed by heights than Connemara, less stern than Donegal. It has more numerous green and happy recesses than either; but these, like Killarney, derive most of their charm from the lonely and dim places behind them. Donegal and Connemara are grim; but in these Highlands, scourged though they are by tempests and thrilled by the perpetual thunder of the heavy waves, you find the first peace that is so akin to the last peace of despair.

O'Sullivan's Punchbowl

THE ISLANDS

Though the Geraldines were strong in their day among the mountains of Kerry, they did not attempt to control the neighbouring islands; nor did any other Normans extend their dominions beyond the brink of the seas. Almost all the many islands within sight of the cliffs of the North and the West remained peculiarly Irish.

This was no doubt due in part to the fact that nobody else wanted them. Even Cromwell, though he decreed that all the islands should be cleared of the Irish, did not try to give them away. And although in later times there was a futile attempt to colonise Achill, off the coast of Mayo, the islands are all left in the hands of the one race eccentric enough to find pleasure in them.

This suited everyone, for the Irish Celt is by nature a lover of islands. Most people would think that Ireland itself was solitary and secluded enough; but that view was not held by the Irish, for there are innumerable remnants of castles and churches and abbeys to be found even on the tiniest of islands in the middle of lakes. Of course some of these were built because the water provided a natural moat. One such was Ross Castle, the O'Donoghue's stronghold in Lough Leane at Killarney, which relied so much on the water around it that a legend arose that the fortress would never be taken till ships of war were afloat on Lough Leane. This prediction was justified by the castle's immunity during many campaigns, and ultimately by its fall, for when the Puritans besieged it they brought boats over the mountains from Bantry to assist their purpose. And this action was indeed of great assistance, for the garrison, trusting in the prophecy, believed instantly that the hour of their doom had arrived and surrendered at once.

GLENA MOUNTAIN, FROM TORC COTTAGE

This was painted at dawn. The body of water is the Middle or Muckross Lake in Killarney.

It was natural that men should enjoy the protection of water in times when every chief was accustomed to amuse himself with midnight raids, or when the English were eagerly pursuing the sport of Hunt the Irish; even the monks could not overlook the advantage of being surrounded by water, since few of their neighbours would have hesitated to burn a church or an abbey if it happened to be under the patronage of someone they disliked. But apart from this, the Celts loved the visible separation of islands. A home on a little island of trees in the heart of a quiet lake hidden by mountains – that was their ideal. There they could live secluded in the care of seclusion, isolated from all the isolation of Ireland.

Those who dwelt on the islands of the savage Atlantic enjoyed, in addition to a greater security, the delight of the contrast afforded by the vain and morose toil of the waves. When Columba introduced music to the worship on rocky Iona, it pleased him to think that it would rise over the tumult of the wind and the surf, and to imagine that sailors, hearing that melody of peace while they struggled in the grip of a storm, would dream that they were listening to the voices of angels. In the same spirit, the primitive monks who were voluntary captives on Aran, Skellig-Michael or smaller rocks found that the rage of the ocean around them lifted their silent and penitential joy. They dedicated the Great Skellig Island to St Michael because they believed that it was his task to restrain the Powers of Darkness; and they loved it the more because its barbarous rim protected a deep hollow of turf. Down in that green cup they formed a Way of the Cross; and if you visit their refuge now, you will see the Stone of Pain and the Rock of the Woman's Wail and the rest where they knelt, when in imagination they followed the path that Christ followed on his way to be crucified at Calvary; and aloft in the wind-beaten cliffs, between the turf and the surf, you will find their separate cells.

Some of these islands have military periods in their history. On Tory Island off Donegal, two African tribes are said to have fought a murderous battle in prehistoric times, beside the Tower of Conning. From Clare Island off Mayo, Grace O'Malley, known as the Sea Queen, dominated all of

THE FOOT OF MANGERTON

This picture gives a good idea, Walker tells us, 'of the way mountain roads often end in stepping stones over a stream, which sometimes becomes a torrent impassable for cars'.

Connemara. She is said to have sailed to England and greeted Queen Elizabeth on equal terms. Other islands were visited by the Danes and the Spaniards and were for a long time the haunts of pirates and wreckers, places of ill-omen to ships. But now they are all peaceful again.

Frank Mathew, describing the islands, reverted to the theme of the isolation of Ireland:

> Many of the islands are a country apart. The people of the Aran Islands follow a primitive form of Christianity, little concerned with later dogmas or pomp; they have laws of their own, and those who infringe them are banished to Ireland; they are mournful and taciturn and full of beliefs more ancient than Dun Aengus, their vast primeval fortification. On Tory Island, the Island of Towers, the people were until recent times accustomed to choosing a king of their own to whom they rendered an implicit obedience. Even now most of the islanders go fishing in coracles, long narrow punts framed of wicker and covered with tarpaulin or skins. It is probable that the early Celts defied the storms in just such vessels as these.

The many islands in the lakes had, of course, no such separate populations. The chiefs who held castles on them enjoyed the seclusion the more because it endured only as long as they liked; they could be hospitable there when they chose, or participate in the battles and the feasts of their neighbours. The monks who built churches on them and little round beehive cells in which they tasted the pleasure of solitude while retaining the other delight of sympathetic companionship were agreeably sundered from life on the shores. They went there to find peace and security in a world of alarms. And now that the castles are all in ruins, the green spots they once overshadowed are as calm as those that hold empty cells and wrecked churches that are left to the dead. Even today some of these islands are places of burial. On Devenish in Lough Erne, a nook on the bank of the lake is still called the

Lough Garagarry

This lough is situated on the lower slope of Mangerton Mountain, Killarney, and forms the end of the wild Glen na Cloghereen. The lough is sometimes called O'Donoghue's Ink Bottle, due to the dark colour of its water.

Port of Lamentation, in memory of the funerals that left it, accompanied by the wild keening of women, when the dead were borne over the water to that island of rest.

It could be said that Ireland is an island of islands, not all of them surrounded by water. Just as in early days it was held by many small nations mutually hostile, so now, after all the violent interventions and compulsory removals, each county has a separate life. In each of them are to be seen distinctions of character; but nonetheless all are Irish. A man whose fathers have lived from time immemorial among reverberating cliffs, condemned to dare the rough Atlantic in coracles, cannot altogether resemble one derived from a family settled in a hushed wilderness of bogs. The accidents of fortune should also be remembered: the subjected and colonised English Pale was bound to differ from intact Donegal.

Yet though they were apart, so was their country. The people of the bogs and the mountains, of the Pale and Donegal, so distinct and disparate in so many ways, are united in their subjection to the magic of Ireland.

Opposite:

CATHEDRAL CLIFFS, ACHILL

These cliffs are accessible only when the tide is out. They are worn into arches and eaves by the action of the water, which has given them a remarkable resemblance to Gothic architecture. On the shaded side

they look sombre and impressive, but when the sun
shines there are varied and brilliant
colours on the lichen rocks.

SAINTS AND SINNERS

It is not certain whether Ireland ought any longer to be called the Island of Saints, but that was a title they chose for themselves long ago, a title they felt was earned by the men and women living in cramped cloisters or going out to instruct the non-believers, teaching the beauty of holiness by their ways and their words. The choice of name suggests that the Irish venerated sanctity, which is why their separate land was sacred to them. The pale hills of Ireland have the beauty of holiness. There is in it the peace of a cloister; it is as quiet as a nun.

The saints of old Ireland were skilled in the invocation of curses; and in this they have always been rivalled by the people, as many traditions show, and as you will probably find if you turn a deaf ear to a beggar. One of the imprecations most commonly employed in the old days by those to whom help was refused was 'Green grow the grass before your door!' It was every Irishman's aim to keep open house and an open heart, and this curse cut him to the quick.

In the old days, the well-to-do gentlemen of Ireland were renowned mainly for three things: hospitality, feasting and duelling. The first involved the second and that was in turn one of the chief causes of the third. But, as Frank Mathew explained, 'You will not understand the old prevalence of duels unless you bear in mind that those meetings were often friendly.'

> They were regulated by laws made in the year 1777 at Clonmel in Tipperary by men representing that county and Galway and Roscommon and Sligo and Mayo. Note that four of these counties

SEAL CAVES, ACHILL

belonged to the Irish Pale. These laws were known as the Galway Code of the Duel. Having enacted that a blow is strictly prohibited under any circumstances amongst gentlemen, they proceeded to indicate how disputes should be settled in an orderly way with pistols or swords. 'No dumb-shooting or firing in the air is admissible in any case,' they decided, for such conduct was 'children's play'. They showed how a man should kill his best friend without a trace of unkindness, for any reason or none. Many of these conflicts were caused, not by mutual hate, but by a common love of danger. There is a good deal to be said for duelling as a form of sport; it must have been more exciting and dangerous than hunting big game, nor did it necessitate journeys to India or Africa; it had a moral influence, for it made men feel the value of a clear eye and a steady hand; above all, it inculcated civility and the importance of an accurate tongue. At the same time, it had some disadvantages. If a man was very proud of his swordsmanship or his knack with a pistol, he might become a public nuisance, a bully or fire-eater.

There is, therefore, reason to think that quite a number of gentlemen usually went to bed sober. But it was not the sober men or the quiet ones who became famous. A man who was grossly intoxicated after drinking a bottle

Opposite:

Cutting Turf

This scene is characteristic of bogland in nearly all parts of Ireland. Francis Walker wrote that although nothing could look more desolate than this bog, 'upon it really depends the existence of the small holders who live on the green patches won from the mountain side'. The turf supplied the only fuel they could get and Walker quoted from a conversation he had with one of the locals: "Well, there is one good thing. Although we are sometimes hungry, we are never cold."

In many instances, the right to cut turf was free to the cottager,
but in some cases, an annual charge was made.

or two of honest wine would have been scorned. Sobriety was esteemed, but only after a fashion. The man who was most respected was he who could drink the most wine without being the worse, for it, he who remained at the table when all his companions were under it. His, said Mathew, 'was a tested sobriety, not a fugitive and cloistered virtue'.

There was a time when all the people of Ireland were pious; but with the increase in civilisation sanctity was left more and more to the rural poor. they were more purely Celtic and more medieval, not being altered by travel or communion with foreigners, and they needed piety more. Their lot in this world was so hard that they were prone to find comfort in dreaming of the joys of the next. These habits of mind were fostered by their certainty that their vicissitudes were directed by Providence and that every temporal sorrow was for their spiritual good, and that the next world would afford compensating delight. If this was so, why should they heed transitory hunger or cold? There is a story of a peasant who had known many calamities, and being asked by a friend whether he wanted anything, answered, 'Only the Day of Judgement.' It was in a similar spirit that the peasants endured many things: there was an inner light that made them forget the dark around. Enlarging on this theme, Mathew wrote:

> That intrinsic piety is still in their hearts. Scratch an Irishman and you will find a saint. You may have to scratch somewhat deep, and I cannot assure you that it will be safe operation, for Irish sanctity has often been militant, like Saint Columba's; but in the least saintly of Irishmen there is the stuff of which martyrs are made.

Opposite:

A Happy Home

'On taking refuge here from a storm,' Walker recalled, 'I was hospitably entertained and when I left, neither the good man nor his wife would take any remuneration whatever. As a small return, I have endeavoured to give their likeness in the happy homestead as I saw it'.